RICKY LAUREN
THE HAMPTONS
Food, Family, and History

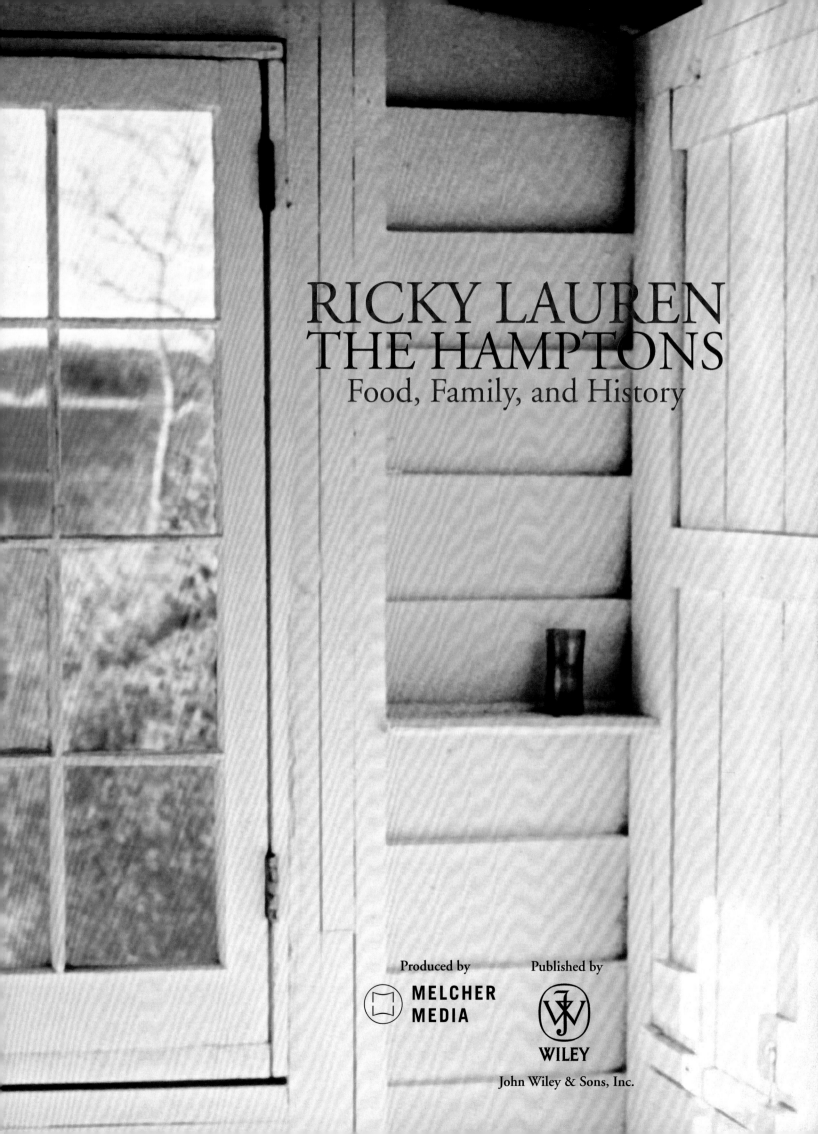

RICKY LAUREN
THE HAMPTONS
Food, Family, and History

Produced by

MELCHER
MEDIA

Published by

WILEY

John Wiley & Sons, Inc.

This book is dedicated to my husband, Ralph—
the captain of our ship and the anchor in my life.

CREATIVE DIRECTION BY RICKY LAUREN

Food Photography by Ann Stratton

Published by John Wiley & Sons, Inc., Hoboken, New Jersey
Published simultaneously in Canada

Produced by MELCHER MEDIA, 124 West 13th Street, New York, NY 10011
www.melcher.com

Charles Melcher, Publisher
Bonnie Eldon, Associate Publisher
Duncan Bock, Editor in Chief

Holly Dolce, Senior Editor
Shoshana Thaler, Associate Editor
Austin O'Malley, Editorial Assistant
Kurt Andrews, Production Director
Daniel Del Valle, Production Associate
Shannon Fanuko, Design Intern

Layout Design by Lynne Yeamans

Food Styling by Michael Pederson
Prop Styling by Philippa Brathwaite

For general information on our other products and services, or technical support, please contact our Customer Care Department within the United States at 800-762-2974, outside the United States at 317-572-3993 or fax 317-572-4002.

Wiley publishes in a variety of print and electronic formats and by print-on-demand. Some material included with standard print versions of this book may not be included in e-books or in print-on-demand. If this book refers to media such as a CD or DVD that is not included in the version you purchased, you may download this material at http://booksupport.wiley.com. For more information about Wiley products, visit www.wiley.com.

Library of Congress Cataloging-in-Publication Data is available upon request.

ISBN: 978-1-118-29327-0

Printed in China
10 9 8 7 6 5 4 3 2 1

CONTENTS

Over the years my family and I have experienced living in four different areas of the Hamptons. We found each one to be unique in environment and lifestyle. When Ralph and I were first married the mood of Southampton, with its architecture of elegant estate-like homes and its establishment restaurants, attracted us as newlyweds who were eager to build a family of our own. Later on we were drawn to Amagansett's casual, barefoot style where families lived in cozy, clustered houses situated along unpaved roads. It was perfect for us with two young boys. When our family grew to be five in number, East Hampton offered us visions of baseball games on beautiful lawns surrounding sprawling family residences.

Eventually we settled in Montauk, the town farthest out on the island and therefore, the most remote and private. Montauk has been described as a fisherman's village, a surfer's community, and an artist's refuge. The homes there are not manicured, but rather more individualistic and simple.

I experienced my own growth as a creator of our home environments while raising my family and seeking my identity as an independent individual. Over the years the type of food and entertaining we enjoyed reflected the atmosphere of the places that we lived in at the time. Each locale inspired me to create a particular way of life, and this energized me to develop a direction of my own.

Contained within these pages are the tried-and-true recipes that we have enjoyed as a family, and which we love to serve to our guests when we entertain. Some recipes were passed down to me by my mother. Others I acquired as a young wife and mother cooking to please my husband and growing family. Many recipes have come from the wonderful and talented chefs who we have been proud to claim as part of our family over the years.

I would like to share the sense of grace and ease that I feel comes with mastering a few basic culinary skills. This book is organized by meals—breakfasts, lunches, starters, dinners, and desserts. Menus illustrate what I like to serve along with these courses. Please consider this book a launching point. Use it to explore your own creativity to find new and exciting ways to combine food to make your family, your guests, and yourself happy!

Ricky Lauren

A Beautiful, Healthy Plate

My family loves color, so we choose our vegetables to paint a beautiful plate. We are also a family that takes health very seriously, so meals are not only colorful but nutritious as well. Our favorite vegetables are broccoli, carrots, Brussels sprouts, beets, and zucchini. They appear frequently throughout this book because of their color palette, their nutritional value, and their flavor.

In the summertime we also love corn—especially the tiny white kernels that burst in your mouth and are as sweet as candy. Fresh peas, arugula, and tender asparagus spears are also high on our list. Broccoli rabe sautéed in garlic and oil has become one of our new favorite vegetables.

A Note on Salads

Just like an artist one can create a colorful textural painting that is visually attractive as well as a tasty adventure for the palette—try your hand at becoming the painter and use what nature has presented to you. Make a compatible dressing that is fresh and light and cheers the diner on to the next course.

And Fruit...

Summertime is the perfect time to add ripe fruit to your salads and to create so many desserts using the bounty of the season.

Here are some of my favorite ways to prepare vegetables:

STEAMING: Steaming vegetables allows them to retain their color, texture, and flavor. You need a large saucepan with a lid and a steamer basket or a colander that fits inside the pan. Fill the pan with just enough water to reach the bottom of the basket or colander. Bring the water to a boil, add the vegetables, and put the lid on. Cooking time depends on the size and thickness of the vegetables: Asparagus will take 4 to 6 minutes, broccoli 5 minutes, carrots 6 to 8 minutes, green beans 5 minutes.

SAUTÉING: This style of high-heat cooking gives vegetables a more concentrated taste. The water in the vegetables evaporates, leaving them tender but crisp. Use a flat-bottom sauté pan. Coat the bottom with oil, butter, or stock. Heat the pan. Cut the vegetables into equal-size pieces. Add the hard ones (carrots, potatoes) to the pan first, then the softer or quicker-cooking ones (zucchini, asparagus). Allow the vegetables to cook undisturbed for several minutes to brown, then toss to keep them from burning. Most vegetables take 3 to 5 minutes to sauté.

GRILLING: Cut vegetables into pieces that will cook evenly, ¾ to 1 inch thick. Soak them in cold water for 20 minutes. Pat dry, brush with oil, and cook for 2 to 3 minutes on each side.

PARBOILING: To "parboil" is to partially cook vegetables in boiling water. You must remove them before they are cooked through and finish by stir-frying or grilling them, or freezing them for later use. This is a great method for preparing carrots, potatoes, and other vegetables that take a little longer to cook and could benefit from being precooked in advance.

ROASTING: Roasting brings out the sweetness in vegetables and is a good way to cook bell peppers (roast whole peppers until blackened and collapsed, then remove the skin and seeds), winter squash, root vegetables, Brussels sprouts, and asparagus. Preheat the oven to 400°F. Wash the vegetables and pat them dry. Cut them into uniform pieces. Put the vegetables in a bowl and toss with a drizzle of olive oil, salt, and pepper. Lightly oil the bottom of a roasting pan and add the vegetables in a single layer. Roast for 10 minutes, then stir, return to the oven, and roast for 10 more minutes. Continue this at 10-minute intervals until the vegetables are nicely browned all over and tender throughout.

Early Hamptons History

The area known as the Hamptons consists of a succession of stylish, popular resort towns starting with Southampton, ninety miles due east of New York City. It continues on for thirty miles through Water Mill, Bridgehampton, Sagaponack, Wainscott, Sag Harbor, East Hampton, Amagansett, the town of Montauk, and six miles beyond to Montauk Point with a lighthouse at its easternmost tip. The Hamptons lie on the South Fork of Long Island on a strip of land that is only ten miles at its widest and is separated from the rest of Long Island by the Shinnecock Canal. The southern shore faces the Atlantic Ocean, and the northern shore—the "bay side"—faces the Great Peconic Bay, Little Peconic Bay, Gardiner's Bay, Napeague Bay, and the Long Island Sound. The varied terrain in between consists of dunes, bays, lakes, ponds, swamps, marshes, pine barrens, farmland, woodlands, high ridges, and rocky cliffs.

Two tribes of the Algonquin Indians inhabited Long Island long before the early settlers arrived. The Shinnecocks and the Montauketts subsisted on a diet of squash, beans, and corn, which they grew in the fertile East End soils. In the winter months they created a porridge out of the corn that they had stored up after the autumn harvest. They also ate fruits and nuts from trees and wild berry bushes. From the bay, they consumed oysters, clams, scallops, whelks, and mussels, which were available in all seasons. Nets, baskets, and forked branches were used to trap fish that were marooned in the pools between the high and low ocean tides. Hooks and harpoons

were fashioned out of deer bones and antlers. The Montauketts became skilled at spearfishing from long, multi-manned dugout canoes in deeper water. They also hunted game in the dense wooded areas farther inland. They were generally a peaceful people.

By the mid-1630s, the Dutch, who had found their way to this continent, had been steadily purchasing land from the Indians. They had acquired Manhattan and most of the area now known as Brooklyn and Queens. In 1640, a small boat from Lynn, Massachusetts, arrived at Conscience Point, Long Island. Its passengers came in search of land on which to establish a plantation and a permanent home. They were led south by the friendly Shinnecocks to the area they named "Old Town," today's Southampton. More small groups of English colonists followed. Agreements and treaties were new to the Indians, but they soon engaged in transactions that included the trading of land for blankets, coats, hatchets, mirrors, knives, wampum, and other prized items.

The town of East Hampton was established in 1648, when thirty-four Puritan families settled on its shores. They had purchased shares of the land from the governors of New Haven and Connecticut, who had previously negotiated for it with the Montaukett Indians.

The early settlers recruited the Indians as laborers. The Indians worked alongside them and demonstrated their methods for planting and harvesting, butchering livestock, and fishing. While the settlers devoted themselves to clearing and working the land for farms and pastures, tradespeople specializing in carpentry, woodworking, blacksmithing, and

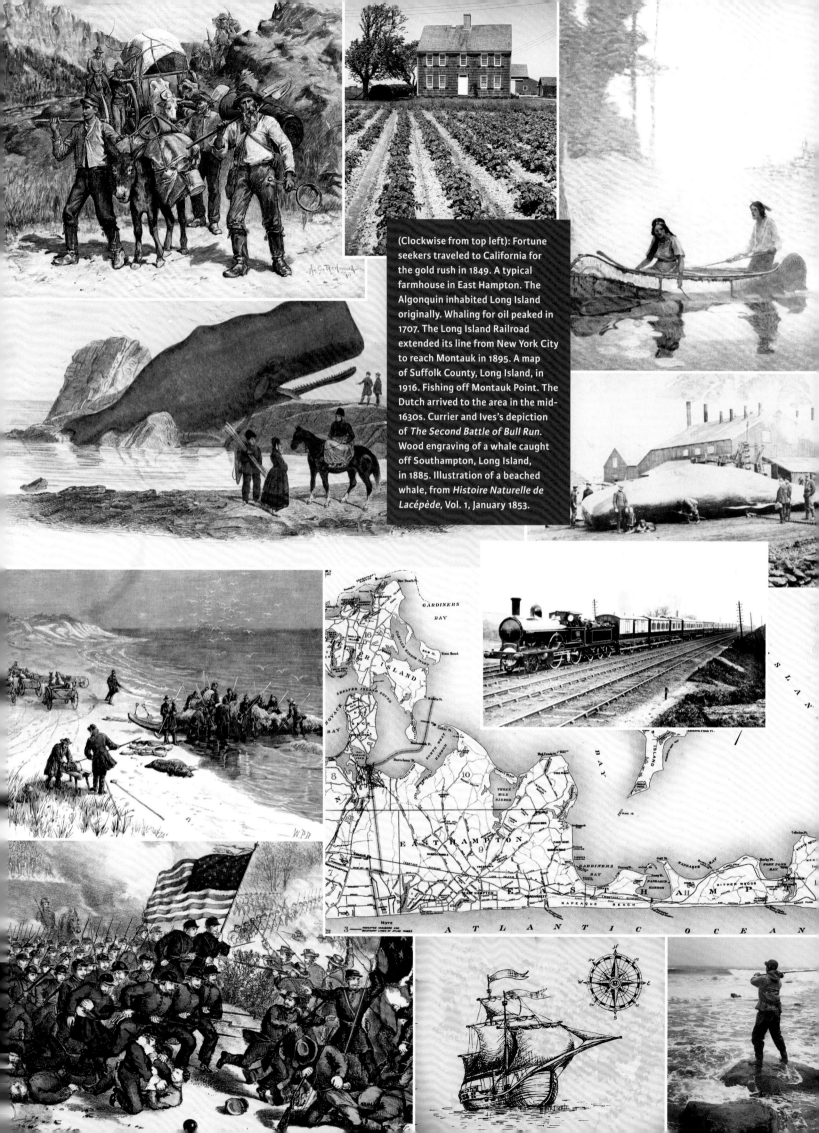

(Clockwise from top left): Fortune seekers traveled to California for the gold rush in 1849. A typical farmhouse in East Hampton. The Algonquin inhabited Long Island originally. Whaling for oil peaked in 1707. The Long Island Railroad extended its line from New York City to reach Montauk in 1895. A map of Suffolk County, Long Island, in 1916. Fishing off Montauk Point. The Dutch arrived to the area in the mid-1630s. Currier and Ives's depiction of *The Second Battle of Bull Run*. Wood engraving of a whale caught off Southampton, Long Island, in 1885. Illustration of a beached whale, from *Histoire Naturelle de Lacépède*, Vol. 1, January 1853.

weaving arrived to perform the necessary labor for the further development of the community. In the 1700s, ranchland for cattle extended over the entire Montauk peninsula. By the 1740s, houses were being built in Montauk. From Southampton to Montauk, the land had taken on the gentle aspect of farms, with abundant pastures for cultivating crops or grazing livestock. All the while, the settlers continued their alliance with the New England colonies. To this day, evidence of that relationship is retained in the look of the buildings in the towns, villages, and hamlets of East Hampton and Southampton, which include Wainscott, Springs, Amagansett, and Montauk.

Early on, the beach was seen as a lonely wasteland of flat expanse and sea wreckage. In those days, whales, highly valued for their oil, were often found beached on the ocean-side shores. Every able-bodied man took part in severing the blubber and extracting the oil. Indian-built canoes that were thirty to thirty-five feet long were manned by the Indians for offshore whaling. By 1675, the settlers had joined the Indians, and whaling moved into even deeper waters. Whaling reached its peak by 1707, when four thousand barrels of oil were collected.

The town of Sag Harbor constructed a seaport in 1730, which became the most important whaling center and the principal port on the northeastern coast by the 1800s, second only to New York City.

In August 1776, during the Revolutionary War, Long Island fell under British occupation. Homes were plundered and cattle were seized by the military. There was little food, since farmers and fishermen from the area had joined Washington's army and abandoned their agrarian pursuits for the dura-

tion of the war. Some inhabitants fled to Connecticut or were taken prisoner.

When the war was finally over, the victorious, now independent colonists could return to their livelihoods and continue to expand on their development of the area. In 1792, George Washington authorized the construction of the Montauk Lighthouse. The area basked in a natural prosperity, for all the way from Southampton to Montauk, herds of cattle and goats could be seen grazing on the land, and fish were abundant in the sea.

By the middle of the 1800s, kerosene had replaced whale oil, and whaling was in decline. Many able-bodied men were attracted to California for the gold rush of 1849–59. The Civil War drew young men from the area to enlist in the Union army. Once again an idyllic lifestyle was interrupted by war. During this time forests were stripped, and natural wildlife such as bear, bobcat, wolf, and wild game disappeared from the area.

When the Civil War ended in 1865, the quiet ways of farming, fishing, and town-building once again resumed. Fishing became the winter occupation of the farmer. The ocean offered up striped bass, black sea bass, salmon, bluefish, flounder, fluke, and cod to be eaten fresh or smoked for consumption later in the year. The bays offered clams, oysters, mussels, lobsters, and scallops. Other fish of lesser quality were used as animal feed and fertilizer.

Craftsmen returned, and new talent arrived in the East Hampton area. Weavers, stonemasons, millers, builders, tailors, and furniture-makers skillfully created what would become precious historical examples of the period's artifacts, furnishings, and buildings.

Perhaps the greatest change was the arrival of the railroad. Before this, Long

Island had been relatively inaccessible to New York City, which was a young and growing metropolis. Travel from New York to East Hampton consisted of a difficult three-day trip by stagecoach. Then in 1844 the railroad connected New York City to Greenport. Travelers had to take the train to one of the stations en route, namely Manorville, and then board a horse-drawn stagecoach to Southampton. In 1870 the South Shore railroad line that reached Southampton was extended to Bridgehampton and linked Sag Harbor to the main line. Finally in 1895, the Long Island Railroad line was extended from Bridgehampton through East Hampton and Amagansett to Montauk.

The railroad boosted tourism. At last people from the big city could venture out to the area more easily to enjoy the invigorating fresh sea air, cooling briny breezes, bright sandy beaches, and sparkling ocean—a respite from city life. Boardinghouses became popular stops for visitors' sojourns. Soon summer homes were built, beach resorts were developed, and commercial traffic increased.

New ethnic and religious groups arrived as well. The Irish, Polish, Italians, and Germans became the new "settlers," bringing their own trades, customs, and idiosyncrasies. In 1873, the first ducks arrived via clipper ship from China (hence the name Peking ducks). Potatoes had been a staple crop of the Sagaponack Indians. The Europeans developed potato growing into a commercial entity, along with fruit growing and duck farming.

In every direction the land boasted farms with fruit-bearing orchards and abundant crops of corn, rye, turnips, and wheat—and endless potato fields. More green pastureland was set aside for grazing cattle and sheep. Long Island had become an agrarian paradise.

In 1907, Hal Fullerton, a special agent for the Long Island Railroad, set up experimental farms to promote agricultural Long Island as the "Garden of Eden." He and his wife, Edith, wanted to prove that anything could be grown there. The Long Island Railroad shipped crates of produce to other parts of the area and to the New York City markets.

Commercial fishing and farming thrived with the new railroad extension. At first, only items that did not need refrigeration were processed and shipped to New York. Once refrigeration became available, fresh produce and boxes of fish were transported on a special fish train and arrived at the Fulton Fish Market early the next morning.

With the coming of the railroad to the Hamptons, the distance from the great cultural center of New York City no longer seemed so great. The combination of this and the simple beauty of the landscape attracted many visitors to the Hamptons. The crashing of the surf on the sandy beaches, dunes with beach grasses blowing in the breezes, seagulls' cries as they soared at random over the sand and the sea, spectacular light, and a chance for solitary, revivifying walks along the beach were all now considerably more accessible and beckoned people to the area.

CHAPTER 1
Southampton

In the early 1970s, we stayed in the Hamptons for the first time. We lived in a converted red barn located behind an elegant white clapboard mansion on a prominent thoroughfare in Southampton. To get home, we had to use a driveway on one side of the main house. After maneuvering our car through some scraggly pines, Rosa rugosa, and overgrown weeds that sprouted between the pebbles, we arrived at a meadow spotted with buttercups and dandelions. In the middle of this fieldlike lawn stood the faded red barn.

Inside, the dark, cavernous living room had two walls that were made of barn siding. There was one entire wall of French casement doors, which let in the late-afternoon sunlight. Each day we opened these doors to greet the delightfully long summer afternoons and the grassy meadow, just a step across the threshold.

Ricky holding Andrew. Southampton, July 1970.

A river-rock fireplace covered an entire river-rock wall, floor to ceiling, and at least twenty people could be seated along its bumpy grouted hearth. We carefully closed the flue after each visit, yet always found various winged creatures waiting to greet us on our next arrival.

Fires in the fireplace were somewhat frightening in their size and fury. Perhaps it was that the logs we used were old and dry. We were young novices working to create the romance and warm atmosphere this wonderful house seemed to deserve.

The ceiling was high. Rafters of thick wooden beams with huge black iron bolts and steel grommets served to support its structure. I was not surprised to discover a bird's nest occupying one of the ledges.

I spent a great deal of time in the red brick–walled kitchen. It wasn't very large, but it had a huge butcher block in its center. The block had been put to extensive use, evident from its uneven surface. It was the kind of stage that evoked past creations of gastronomic excess and served as an inspiration for me to create my own style of summer fare for family and friends.

A number of enormously heavy French copper pots and pans hung by their handles from an iron rack. I climbed a rickety old wooden ladder to get them down to cook our meals. I finally brought my own more manageable kitchenware, including utensils that I could wield kung fu–style.

The sink was old and deep enough for arranging a field of flowers, or even giving a large dog a bath. It came in handy for scrubbing those copper pots. In those days, our first child, Andrew, was with us, and I enjoyed bathing him in that giant sink. The butcher block was perfect as Andrew's dressing table.

In our family history, this was the summer when I expanded my cooking skills and Andrew learned to walk. I remember how Ralph would hold up a broomstick horizontally, and Andrew would cling to it with both hands. Ralph would slowly step backward and Andrew, knuckles paling, would uncertainly teeter left to right and finally take one tentative step forward. Then the second foot would bravely catch up to the first, and Andrew was balanced less precariously once again.

Ralph with beard and mustache! July 1970.

Andrew (age 1) and Ricky, July 1970.

Andrew riding his tricycle, July 1970.

And so it continued, step by step, teetering and tottering, while Ralph patiently took mini steps backward. I remember Andrew becoming jubilant, beaming with each excited paternal compliment. This continued on and on for days and days, until "hooray," the stick was abandoned and the glorious accomplishment was proclaimed throughout the land. I, too, was relishing my accomplishments as, slowly but surely, my culinary skills developed. We were all inspired by the atmosphere of this somewhat formal yet rustic Southampton kitchen, and we savored our family life there.

Breakfasts

Chopped Mushroom, Spinach, and Cheddar Omelette

Ricky's Cinnamon and Vanilla Challah French Toast
Served with Fresh Berries

Individual Iron-Skillet Sunny-Side-Up Eggs with Smoked
Salmon Rosettes and Toasted Sourdough Bread

Chopped Mushroom, Spinach, and Cheddar Omelette

1 teaspoon unsalted butter

½ cup chopped cremini mushrooms

4 large eggs, well beaten

Salt and freshly ground black pepper

½ cup cooked spinach, well drained and chopped

2 tablespoons grated cheddar cheese

Heat the butter in an omelette pan over medium heat and lightly sauté the mushrooms. Season the eggs with salt and pepper and add them to the pan; cook without stirring until the bottom is set. Lift the eggs with a silicone spatula so that uncooked egg can flow underneath and cook. Top with the spinach and cheese and fold in half. Serve immediately.

SERVES 2

Ricky's Cinnamon and Vanilla Challah French Toast
Served with Fresh Berries

I love to start my family's day at the beach with this lovely, warm, delicious breakfast. If I can sell seconds to them, then I am the Queen of the Kitchen! I use an egg challah. I cut it 1 inch thick and as much on the diagonal as possible to get the largest slices. French toast is best when it's crispy and golden on the outside and rich and custardy on the inside. The trick is for the bread to soak up the maximum egg mixture without falling apart in the pan. I love the smell of the vanilla and the sound of bread frying. Top it with cinnamon or powdered sugar, then berries on top for the visual effect after plating. You may also present this with grape jelly, strawberry preserves, a "honey bear," and a bowl of cinnamon sugar on the side.

6 large eggs

3 cups low-fat milk

2 teaspoons vanilla extract

Pinch of salt

12 (1-inch-thick) slices day-old challah bread, cut diagonally

Unsalted butter

Safflower or canola oil

Cinnamon sugar or confectioners' sugar

Syrup or jam or honey

Preheat the oven to 250°F.

Beat the eggs, milk, vanilla, and salt together in a large bowl until cream-colored. Pour into a shallow dish. Dip the bread in the mixture, one slice at a time, until soaked.

Sweep a stick of butter around the inside of a hot oiled skillet. Fry the bread in batches over medium heat until golden brown, turning once, about 3 to 4 minutes on each side. Remove to a baking sheet in the oven to keep warm until all the slices are cooked. Serve sprinkled with cinnamon sugar and syrup.

SERVES 6

Individual Iron-Skillet Sunny-Side-Up Eggs
with Smoked Salmon Rosettes and Toasted Sourdough Bread

I love the way a pair of bright yellow-and-white eggs look frying against the pure blackness of the iron skillet. Farm-fresh organic eggs are best. As for the skillets, choose a size that fits two eggs so that each diner can have his or her own pan—the feeling of immediacy that comes from eating the eggs directly from the pan enhances the meal.

Salted butter

2 fresh eggs per person

Salt and freshly ground
black pepper

Thin slices of Nova Scotia salmon
(lox), or crisp cooked bacon

Sliced sourdough bread

Jelly and preserves

For each diner, heat a small cast-iron skillet over medium heat. Add the butter, and when it melts, crack in the eggs. Season with salt and pepper to taste and cook until the white is set and the yolk has thickened slightly. Serve the eggs in the pan. Roll up the salmon slices and serve them (or the bacon) alongside, with bread and pots of jelly and preserves.

Luncheon

Summer Garden Vegetable Pie

Rising Tide Lobster Soufflé

Open-Faced Sandwich of Smoked Salmon and
Sliced Cucumber on a Loaf of Pumpernickel

Pasta with Hamptons Summer Vegetables

Summer Garden Vegetable Pie

This delicious pie is a versatile summer lunch dish, or it can be a starter, or a side dish for a dinner. As a lunch, it can stand on its own with a garden vegetable salad dressed in a light vinaigrette. I like to serve more than one type of salad at lunchtime with this pie, as well as a cup of soup. It is a wonderful accompaniment to a protein, such as an organic chicken breast, sliced turkey, grilled fish, seafood, or fish cakes. For an entirely new slant, this basic pie can be made with chicken, turkey, or seafood as its main ingredient instead of vegetables. A vegetarian pie, as well as a pie with shrimp or chicken, at the noon meal makes everyone happy!

FOR THE CRUST

½ cup (1 stick) unsalted butter

2½ cups all-purpose flour

1 tablespoon baking powder

1 teaspoon salt

1 cup cold buttermilk

1 tablespoon butter, melted

FOR THE FILLING

2 cups broccoli and/or cauliflower florets, steamed until tender-crisp

½ cup diced onion

½ cup diced red or green bell pepper

½ cup grated cheddar cheese

1 teaspoon salt

¼ teaspoon freshly ground black pepper

3 large eggs, beaten

1½ cups milk

¾ cup biscuit mix

Preheat the oven to 475°F.

TO MAKE THE CRUST: Cut the butter into small cubes and freeze for 15 to 20 minutes. Stir the dry ingredients together in a large bowl. Add in the butter (using your fingers is best) until the mixture resembles a coarse meal. Stir in the buttermilk until a dough forms. Knead for 3 to 4 turns on a lightly floured surface, and then mold the dough into a nonstick 9-inch pie pan with the edges overlapping. Brush the crust with the melted butter.

TO MAKE THE FILLING: Chop the broccoli and/or cauliflower into small pieces. In a large bowl, combine the broccoli, cauliflower, onion, bell pepper, cheese, salt, and pepper. Combine the eggs, milk, and biscuit mix in a separate bowl and beat well. Add the vegetable mixture and combine thoroughly. Pour into the crust and cook until firm in the center and golden on top, about 40 minutes. Slice and serve hot.

SERVES 4

Rising Tide Lobster Soufflé

I was lucky enough to learn how to make a soufflé from a French chef. The secret to a successful soufflé is to separate the eggs and whip the air, or "breath"—*souffle* is the French word for breath—into the whites. Once you've mastered a soufflé, you can investigate doing anything with it. Make it savory or sweet, big or small.

3 tablespoons unsalted butter, plus more for greasing dish

3 tablespoons all-purpose flour

1 cup whole milk

2 tablespoons vegetable oil

¼ cup chopped onion

¼ cup chopped carrot

¼ cup chopped celery

2 cups lobster meat, chopped and boiled

2 tablespoons sherry

4 egg yolks

5 egg whites

Preheat the oven to 425°F.

Melt the butter in a skillet over medium heat. Add the flour and stir constantly for 2 minutes. Add the milk all at once and stir until smooth, thick, and bubbly, 4 to 5 minutes. Remove from heat and set aside.

In a separate pan, heat the oil and sauté the onion, carrot, and celery together until tender. Add the lobster and sherry. Combine with soufflé sauce. Allow to cool.

Beat the egg yolks and add them to the mixture. In a clean bowl, whip the egg whites. Fold one-third of the whites into the mixture. Then fold the mixture into the remaining whites. Pour into a buttered 8-inch soufflé dish and bake until puffed and golden, approximately 35 minutes.

SERVES 4

Open-Faced Sandwich of Smoked Salmon
and Sliced Cucumber on a Loaf of Pumpernickel

When I was a little girl I went on a trip to Vienna with my parents in the summertime. During that trip my mother took me to a farm outside of the city. The farm had orchards and livestock. The farmer's wife baked fresh bread every morning that was served at the 10 a.m. snack break. She would cut generous slices of bread and present them as open-faced sandwiches with various toppings. Basically each slice had a different farm-style hors d'oeuvre. As a child I was not happy with the toppings made out of fish, so my pumpernickel was slathered with a blend of cream cheese and chopped vegetables. No matter what the topping, an open-faced sandwich is so pretty to look at!

2 scallions, chopped

8 ounces whipped cream cheese

12 slices pumpernickel bread, lightly toasted

8 ounces smoked salmon

6 small ripe tomatoes, very thinly sliced

1 English cucumber, very thinly sliced

Sprigs of fresh dill

Red leaf lettuce, washed and torn into bite-size pieces

½ jicama, julienned

2 tablespoons capers

Mix the scallions into the cream cheese. Spread each slice of bread generously with the mixture. Arrange the salmon, tomatoes, and cucumber decoratively on each sandwich and garnish with dill. Cut the sandwiches diagonally into quarters (from corner to corner). Place a handful of lettuce on each plate, and arrange the sandwiches on top, along with the jicama and capers.

SERVES 6

Pasta with Hamptons Summer Vegetables

For this recipe I always use the freshest, youngest, and most tender vegetables that are available in season. Growing them yourself or picking them up at a local farmstand is the most fun. I enjoy gathering baby peas bursting from their pods, sweet baby carrots, ripe tomatoes, and young, proud green-and-white asparagus spears, to which I add tender zucchini. I always marvel at the colorful selection in my basket. Generally, I combine the fresh vegetables with a delicate pasta like angel hair (capellini). Everybody likes this light spring/summer meal. Add a simple salad and a crusty breadstick and enjoy!

2 tablespoons olive oil

½ cup pine nuts

2 cloves garlic, minced

1 cup sliced white mushrooms

1 cup sliced zucchini (yellow and green), lightly steamed

1 cup broccoli florets, lightly steamed

1½ cups baby carrots, lightly steamed

6 green-and-white asparagus spears, sliced and lightly steamed

1 cup snap peas

1 cup grape tomatoes, halved

¾ cup chopped fresh basil

Salt and pepper

⅔ cup heavy cream

2 cups grated Parmesan cheese

1 pound capellini, cooked

In a large saucepan, over medium heat, add the oil and sauté the pine nuts and garlic until golden brown, 2 to 3 minutes.

Add the mushrooms and sauté for 2 to 3 minutes. Add the steamed vegetables, peas, tomatoes, a half cup of the basil, and salt and pepper to taste. Cook until the vegetables are heated.

Stir in the cream, 1 cup of the Parmesan, and the remaining one-quarter cup basil. Serve over the pasta, accompanied with the remaining 1 cup of Parmesan for sprinkling.

SERVES 4 TO 6

First Courses

Cheese Soufflés

Curried Butternut Squash-and-Apple Soup

Heirloom Tomato and Mozzarella Tart

Spinach Soup with Challah Croutons

Viennese Cucumber Salad

Asparagus, Mushroom, and Red Pepper Quiche

Steamers and Crisp Garlic Bread

Cheese Soufflés

My family loves the Goat Cheese Soufflé served in the Spring Pea Soup (see page 96). Both of these also shine when served on their own.

Gruyère Cheese Soufflé

1 cup dry bread crumbs
(to coat ramekins)

3 tablespoons unsalted butter

3 tablespoons all-purpose flour

¼ cup whole milk

4 large eggs, separated

1 cup grated Gruyère cheese

1 cup freshly grated
Parmesan cheese

¼ teaspoon freshly grated
nutmeg

Salt and freshly ground
black pepper

Preheat the oven to 400°F.

Butter six (¾-cup) ramekins and sprinkle with the bread crumbs. In a saucepan, melt the butter and add the flour. Cook the roux over medium heat for 2 minutes, stirring constantly. Remove from heat and gradually whisk in the milk. Return to medium heat and boil for 3 to 4 minutes. Slowly add the egg yolks. Add the cheeses and nutmeg, and season with salt and pepper to taste.

In a bowl, beat the egg whites until soft peaks form. Gently fold the whites into the sauce. Pour into the prepared soufflé dishes until ¾ full and bake until browned and puffed, 8 to 10 minutes. Serve immediately.

SERVES 6

Goat Cheese Soufflé

½ cup dry bread crumbs

2 tablespoons unsalted
butter

2 tablespoons
all-purpose flour

⅔ cup whole milk

5 ounces goat cheese,
crumbled

½ teaspoon salt

¼ teaspoon freshly
ground black pepper

2 large egg yolks, whisked

4 large egg whites

Preheat the oven to 350°F.

Butter six (¾-cup) ramekins and coat them with the bread crumbs. Melt the butter in a saucepan over low heat. Add the flour and cook the roux for 2 minutes, whisking constantly. Gradually whisk in the milk. Increase the heat to medium and simmer until the mixture thickens, stirring constantly, about 5 minutes. Add the cheese and whisk until melted. Add the salt and pepper. Gradually whisk the egg yolks into the soufflé base and let the mixture cool.

Beat the egg whites in a large bowl until stiff but not dry. Stir one-quarter of the whites into the soufflé base to lighten it. Fold in the remaining whites. Divide the mixture among the ramekins and place them in a 9-by-13-inch baking pan. Add enough hot water to the pan to come halfway up the sides of the ramekins.

Bake until puffed and golden brown on top and set in the center, about 20 minutes. Serve the soufflés in the middle of the Spring Pea Soup.

SERVES 6

Curried Butternut Squash-and-Apple Soup

2 tablespoons unsalted butter

1 tablespoon olive oil

1 medium onion, chopped

1 tablespoon curry powder

2 tablespoons grated fresh ginger, or ½ teaspoon ground dried ginger

¼ teaspoon ground cardamom

1 medium butternut squash, peeled, seeded, and chopped

5 cups chicken stock

2 large apples (preferably a mixture of Granny Smith and Jonagold), peeled, cored, and chopped

Juice of 1 lemon

1 cup apple cider

Salt and freshly ground black pepper

6 tablespoons plain yogurt

Heat the butter and oil in a large saucepan over medium heat. Add the onion, curry powder, ginger, and cardamom and cook for 2 minutes. Add the squash and cook for 5 minutes, stirring.

Add the stock, apples, lemon juice, and cider and cook until the squash is fork-tender, 20 minutes. Season to taste with salt and pepper.

Puree the soup with an immersion blender or in batches in a blender. Serve warm or chilled, with 1 tablespoon of the yogurt in the center of each serving.

SERVES 6

Heirloom Tomato and Mozzarella Tart

This tart can be a light lunch or a delicious first course.

FOR THE CRUST

½ cup all-purpose flour

½ cup whole wheat flour

¼ teaspoon salt

½ teaspoon freshly ground black pepper

2 cups (8 ounces) freshly grated Parmesan cheese

½ cup (1 stick) unsalted butter, chilled and diced

2 to 3 tablespoons ice-cold water

FOR THE FILLING

1½ cups grated mozzarella (6 ounces)

6 mixed-color heirloom tomatoes, washed and sliced ¼ inch thick

¼ cup roughly chopped fresh basil

1 tablespoon chopped fresh oregano

3 tablespoons chopped scallion greens

2 tablespoons olive oil

Preheat the oven to 375°F.

TO MAKE THE CRUST: Put the flours, salt, pepper, Parmesan, and butter in a food processor. Pulse until the mixture resembles coarse meal. With the motor running, drizzle in the water until the dough starts to stick together.

Press the dough into a 9- to 10-inch tart pan with a removable bottom. Place in the refrigerator for about 15 minutes.

Prick the bottom of the crust all over with a fork. Line with parchment paper and then fill with pie weights or dried beans. Bake in the center of the oven for about 15 minutes. Remove the parchment and weights, and return the pastry shell to the oven to bake until golden, 15 minutes longer. Let cool completely. Reduce oven to 350°F.

TO MAKE THE FILLING: Sprinkle one-third of the mozzarella over the bottom of the pastry shell. Arrange one-third of the tomato slices on top of the cheese. Sprinkle with one-third of the basil, oregano, and scallion greens. Repeat this step two more times, then drizzle with the oil.

Bake until the mozzarella has melted, 15 to 20 minutes, and serve hot or at room temperature on fresh baby arugula with grape tomatoes.

SERVES 4 TO 6

Spinach Soup
with Challah Croutons

FOR THE SOUP

1 medium onion, chopped

2 cloves garlic, crushed

1 tablespoon olive oil

2 (8-ounce) packages baby spinach

1 quart chicken stock

Fresh basil

FOR THE CROUTONS

1 loaf challah bread

Melted butter

Clove of chopped garlic

1 teaspoon freshly chopped parsley

TO MAKE THE SOUP: Sauté the onion and garlic in the oil until soft and translucent. Add both packages of spinach. Sauté until wilted. Add the chicken stock. Bring to a boil. Puree. Serve warm or chilled with the challah croutons and a sprig of fresh basil as a garnish.

TO MAKE THE CROUTONS: (These can be made in advance.) Cut the challah into slices. Remove the crusts and cut the bread into 1½-by-3-inch pieces. Brush with melted butter and the garlic, sprinkle with chopped parsley, and toast in a 400°F oven until crunchy and golden, 5 minutes on each side.

SERVES 6

Viennese Cucumber Salad

4 large cucumbers,
peeled and seeded

2 teaspoons salt

½ tablespoon white
wine vinegar

1 teaspoon sugar

½ teaspoon paprika

Slice the cucumbers vertically as thinly as possible and put them in a large bowl. Add the remaining ingredients and toss to combine. Cover and refrigerate overnight. Serve chilled.

SERVES 6

Asparagus, Mushroom, and Red Pepper Quiche

FOR THE SHORTCRUST
PASTRY

1½ cups all-purpose flour

Pinch of salt

6 tablespoons unsalted
butter, cut into ¼-inch cubes

1 large egg yolk

2 teaspoons cold water

FOR THE FILLING

4 large eggs

½ cup heavy cream

4 ounces (1 cup) Parmesan
cheese, grated

12 asparagus tips, blanched

6 cremini mushrooms, sliced
and lightly sautéed in butter

1 red bell pepper,
cut into strips

Salt and freshly ground
black pepper

Freshly grated nutmeg
(optional)

Preheat the oven to 350°F.

TO MAKE THE SHORTCRUST PASTRY: Put the flour, salt, and butter in a food processor and pulse until the mixture resembles bread crumbs. While still pulsing, add the egg yolk and water, a little at a time, until the mixture comes together.

Roll out the dough on a floured surface and fit it into a 9-inch pie pan. Line with parchment and pie weights or dried beans. Bake for 10 minutes. Let cool. Leave the oven on.

TO MAKE THE FILLING: Whisk the eggs and cream together in a large bowl. Stir in the cheese, asparagus, mushrooms, and bell pepper and season with salt, pepper, and nutmeg to taste.

Pour the mixture into the cooled pie shell. Bake until the top is golden brown and the custard is set, 30 to 35 minutes. Serve hot.

SERVES 6

Viennese Cucumber Salad

Steamers

1 cup cornmeal

½ teaspoon salt

1 pound steamer clams

4 cloves garlic, chopped

2 tablespoons olive oil

¼ cup dry white wine

¼ cup water

2 tablespoons finely chopped fresh parsley

Stir the cornmeal into a pot of cold salted water. Add the clams and soak for about 4 hours. Scrub the clams, discarding any that have already opened.

In a large pot over medium heat, sauté the garlic in the oil. Drain the clams and add them to the pot. Add the wine and ¼ cup water. Turn the heat to low, cover, and steam until the majority of the clams have opened, between 10 to 15 minutes. Discard any clams that have not yet opened. Serve in bowls with the broth, sprinkled with parsley.

SERVES 4

Crisp Garlic Bread

1 loaf French bread

½ cup (1 stick) salted butter

4 cloves garlic, minced

¼ cup finely chopped fresh flat-leaf parsley

1 cup shredded sharp cheddar cheese (optional)

Preheat the broiler. Cut the bread in half lengthwise. Melt the butter in a small saucepan. Add the garlic and parsley. Cook for 3 to 5 minutes.

Brush the bread with the butter mixture. Broil the bread until it's lightly golden brown on top. For an additional indulgence, melt the shredded sharp cheddar on the bread. Slice diagonally into 1-inch pieces.

SERVES 6 TO 8

Main Courses and Side Dishes

Roasted Breast of Veal Stuffed with Mushrooms and Spinach

Sautéed Mélange of Mushrooms

Garlic and Parsley Roasted Rack of Lamb

Sweet Potato Fries

Sautéed Breast of Chicken with Port Wine and Mushroom Sauce

Asparagus Risotto

Cornish Game Hen in Port Wine Sauce with Wild Rice
and Cherry Stuffing

Barely Breaded Fillet of Sole

Pan-Seared Salmon with Roasted Corn and Tomato Salsa

Starry Night Steamed Lobster with Lemon Wedges and Melted Butter

Saffron Risotto with Shrimp and Clams

Vegetarian Lasagna Corral

Stuffed Cabbage with Tomato Sauce

Roasted Breast of Veal
Stuffed with Mushrooms and Spinach

I like to begin this meal with my Curried Butternut Squash-and-Apple Soup (see page 41) and serve it with a Sautéed Mélange of Mushrooms. I love mushrooms.

3 tablespoons olive oil

1 onion, chopped

1 cup sliced cremini mushrooms

1 cup sliced shiitake mushrooms

1 cup sliced button mushrooms

2 cloves garlic, chopped

1 (3- to 4-pound) breast of veal, ribs removed, butterflied (ask your butcher to do this)

Salt and freshly ground black pepper

2 cups fresh spinach

Preheat the oven to 425°F.

Heat the oil in a medium sauté pan over medium heat and sauté the onion, mushrooms, and garlic until tender. Cool to room temperature.

Lay the veal flat on a work surface and season it with salt and pepper. Put the spinach on top of the meat, followed by the mushroom mixture. Roll it up tightly and tie with kitchen string. Roast until a meat thermometer reads 145°F, 30 to 35 minutes. Let the meat rest for 10 to 15 minutes, then slice and serve.

SERVES 6

Sautéed Mélange of Mushrooms

2 teaspoons extra-virgin olive oil

2 teaspoons unsalted butter

2 shallots, minced

2 cloves garlic, minced

8 ounces cremini mushrooms, washed, trimmed, and sliced

1 large portobello mushroom, washed, trimmed, and diced

8 ounces chanterelle mushrooms, washed, trimmed, and halved

8 ounces shiitake mushrooms, washed, trimmed, and quartered

4 ounces porcini mushrooms, washed, trimmed, and sliced

1 tablespoon fresh thyme leaves, or ¼ teaspoon dried thyme

Salt and freshly ground black pepper

Heat the oil and butter in a skillet over medium heat. Add the shallots and garlic and sauté until translucent, about 5 minutes. Add all the mushrooms and sauté until soft and cooked, 5 minutes. Add the thyme and season with salt and pepper to taste. Serve hot.

SERVES 6

Garlic and Parsley Roasted Rack of Lamb

As a young cook I was impressed by the sophistication of a rack of lamb served as the main event at an elegant dinner party. I still think that rack of lamb can be impressive, and I like to serve it with crispy sweet potato fries and baby spinach lightly sautéed with garlic and olive oil.

1 cup panko or French bread crumbs

2 tablespoons minced garlic

¼ cup minced fresh parsley

1 teaspoon salt

1½ teaspoons freshly ground black pepper

4 tablespoons olive oil

2 (8-rib) racks of lamb, trimmed and Frenched (cut away from the end of the chop, so that part of the bone is exposed)

Preheat the oven to 450°F and put an oven rack in the center.

Combine the bread crumbs, garlic, parsley, salt, pepper, and 2 tablespoons of the oil. Heat the remaining 2 tablespoons of oil in a skillet and sear the lamb on all sides. Let the meat rest on a plate for 3 to 4 minutes. Brush the lamb with the bread crumb mixture, coating evenly. Cover the ends of the bones with aluminum foil and place the racks, bone-side down, in a roasting pan. Roast for 12 to 18 minutes, to the desired degree of doneness. Remove from the oven and cover loosely with foil. Allow to rest for 5 to 7 minutes before carving and serving.

SERVES 6 TO 8

Sweet Potato Fries

Canola oil for deep-frying

4 sweet potatoes

2 tablespoons rice flour

2 tablespoons tapioca starch

2 tablespoons cornstarch

2 tablespoons sugar

¼ teaspoon chili powder

¼ teaspoon turmeric

¼ teaspoon sweet paprika

Salt to taste

In a heavy pot, heat the oil to 170°F. Line a baking sheet with parchment paper. Peel the sweet potatoes and cut them into finger-size sticks. Combine all the remaining ingredients except the salt in a large bowl. Toss the sweet potato sticks (one handful at a time) in the dry mixture to coat them. Put the coated sweet potatoes in a sieve. Hold the sieve over the bowl and shake to remove excess coating.

When the oil is hot, working in small batches, add the sweet potatoes and cook until soft. Do not overcook, and do not crowd the pot. Remove the sweet potatoes with a slotted spoon. Drain in a single layer on a paper towel, then transfer the sweet potatoes to the prepared baking sheet. Again, do not crowd the sweet potatoes on the sheet. Freeze for at least 2 hours, longer if possible.

When ready to finish cooking, heat fresh oil to 350°F. Working in batches, deep-fry the frozen sweet potatoes until crisp, 1½ to 2 minutes. Remove them from the oil with a slotted spoon, and drain on fresh paper towels. Season with salt to taste. Serve immediately.

SERVES 4

Sautéed Breast of Chicken
with Port Wine and Mushroom Sauce

I like to serve this recipe with Asparagus Risotto and begin the meal with my Heirloom Tomato and Mozzarella Tart (see page 42).

3 tablespoons olive oil

2 tablespoons salted butter

1½ cups white mushrooms, halved and thinly sliced

Salt and freshly ground black pepper

¾ cup port wine

1 shallot, chopped

¾ cup chicken stock

3 cloves garlic, chopped

1 cup heavy cream

4 boneless, skinless chicken breast halves

Heat 1 tablespoon of the olive oil and 1 tablespoon of the butter in a skillet over medium heat. Add the sliced mushrooms and salt and pepper to taste. Sauté until lightly browned. Transfer the mushrooms to a bowl.

Add the wine and shallot to the same skillet and bring to a boil. Add the stock and continue to cook for 2 minutes.

Add the garlic and cream, then return the mushrooms to the pan and simmer over medium heat, stirring until the sauce is thick enough to coat the spoon, about 5 minutes. Remove from heat.

Sprinkle the chicken with salt and pepper on both sides. Heat the remaining 2 tablespoons olive oil and 1 tablespoon butter in a large, heavy skillet over medium-high heat. Add the chicken and sauté, pressing it occasionally with a slotted spatula, 5 minutes per side. Serve with the mushroom-and-wine sauce.

SERVES 4

Asparagus Risotto

6 cups vegetable or chicken stock

¼ cup olive oil

3 shallots, finely chopped

1 cup Arborio rice

3 to 4 tablespoons white wine

2 cups asparagus tips

½ teaspoon white truffle oil (optional)

2 tablespoons unsalted butter

4 tablespoons finely grated Parmesan cheese (about 1 ounce)

1 teaspoon chopped fresh chives

2 tablespoons chopped fresh parsley

Salt and freshly ground black pepper

Bring the stock to a boil in a saucepan over medium heat. Lower the heat and keep at a simmer.

Heat the olive oil in a saucepan, add the shallots, and sauté for 1 to 2 minutes. Add the rice, stirring to coat with the oil. Add the wine and bring to a simmer. Add the simmering stock ¾ cup at a time, simmering and stirring frequently, making sure that the stock is absorbed before adding more, until the rice is just tender, about 20 minutes.

Add the asparagus with the last addition of stock to allow it to cook and warm through. Remove from heat. Stir in the truffle oil (if using), butter, cheese, chives, and parsley. Season with salt and pepper to taste. Serve warm.

SERVES 4 TO 6

Cornish Game Hen
in Port Wine Sauce with Wild Rice and Cherry Stuffing

I think that the perfect beginning to this meal is the Spinach Soup with Challah Croutons (see page 45).

FOR THE PORT WINE SAUCE

3 tablespoons salted butter

1 large shallot, finely chopped

2 cloves garlic, minced

1½ cups tawny port

3 sprigs fresh thyme

2½ cups chicken or vegetable stock

1 ounce dried porcini mushrooms

Salt and freshly ground black pepper

2 tablespoons all-purpose flour

1 teaspoon balsamic vinegar

FOR THE STUFFING

¾ cup cooked wild rice

¼ cup minced shallots

3 cloves garlic, minced

½ cup dried cherries

2 teaspoons fresh thyme leaves, or ½ teaspoon dried thyme

1 tablespoon unsalted butter, melted

TO MAKE THE PORT WINE SAUCE: Melt 1 tablespoon of the butter in a large saucepan. Add the shallot and garlic and sauté until translucent, about 5 minutes. Add the port and thyme and bring to a boil over high heat. Lower the heat and simmer until reduced to the consistency of syrup, about 30 minutes. Remove and discard the thyme.

Meanwhile, bring the stock to a simmer in a small saucepan. Remove from the heat. Add the mushrooms and let them soak until reconstituted, 10 to 15 minutes. Remove the mushrooms from the liquid using a slotted spoon. When cool, dice the mushrooms. Strain the soaking liquid through a coffee filter to remove sediment.

Add the strained soaking liquid and the mushrooms to the port reduction and bring to a boil. Lower the heat and simmer until reduced to about 1⅓ cups, about 15 minutes. Strain the sauce through a fine-mesh sieve and season with salt and pepper to taste. (At this point, sauce can be refrigerated in an airtight container for up to 2 days.)

Bring the sauce to a low simmer, stirring.

In a small bowl, combine the flour and remaining butter to make a paste. Add to the sauce while whisking rapidly. Continue whisking until the sauce has a smooth consistency, about 2 minutes. Bring to a gentle boil, whisking constantly, and boil for 2 to 3 minutes. Stir in the vinegar and check the seasoning, adding more salt and pepper if needed. Keep warm, or reheat gently when serving.

TO MAKE THE STUFFING: In a small bowl, combine the rice, shallots, garlic, cherries, thyme, and butter. Season with salt and pepper.

FOR THE HENS

6 Cornish game hens, rinsed and patted dry

Salt and freshly ground black pepper

TO MAKE THE HENS: Preheat the oven to 350°F. Season the hens with salt and pepper inside the cavity and all over the outside. Fill the hens with the stuffing.

Place the hens on a rack in a baking dish. Roast in the center of the oven, basting every 10 to 15 minutes, until cooked through, about 50 minutes. Remove from the oven and let rest for 10 to 15 minutes. Cut the hens in half lengthwise and place on an ovenproof serving platter; cover with aluminum foil.

Return the platter to the oven to reheat for about 4 to 5 minutes before serving. Pour the sauce over the hens and serve.

SERVES 6

Barely Breaded Fillet of Sole

Here is a simple way to make fried fish lighter and more healthful—and perhaps even to sell it to the children at the table. Bread the fish on one side only! It's crispy and delightful, and has fewer calories and a more delicate taste. Begin the meal with a soufflé (see page 39) and serve the fish with steamed chopped spinach.

½ cup all-purpose flour

Lawry's garlic salt

6 (6-ounce) fillets of sole

2 large eggs, beaten

1 cup panko bread crumbs

1 cup oil

Lemon wedges

Season the flour to taste with the garlic salt. Dredge one side of each fillet in the flour. Dip the floured side of each fillet in the eggs, then coat the same side with bread crumbs.

Heat the oil in a skillet and fry the uncoated side of the sole first, until the fish turns white. Flip the fish over and fry until golden brown. Transfer to a platter and serve with lemon wedges.

SERVES 4

Pan-Seared Salmon
with Roasted Corn and Tomato Salsa

So pretty and colorful. Consider beginning this meal with an equally colorful salad. We love a salad of baby spinach, avocado, tomatoes, shaved Romano cheese, and pine nuts.

FOR THE CORN AND TOMATO SALSA

2 tablespoons olive oil

3 ears corn, shucked and silks removed

2 cups diced plum tomatoes

¼ cup minced red or sweet onion

1 teaspoon seeded and minced jalapeño pepper

2 tablespoons chopped fresh cilantro (optional)

Juice of ½ lime

Salt and freshly ground black pepper

FOR THE SALMON

6 skin-on salmon fillets, each about 6 ounces and 1½ inches thick

Salt and freshly ground black pepper

2 tablespoons vegetable oil

TO MAKE THE SALSA: Preheat a grill and brush the grate with the oil. Grill the corn for 1 to 2 minutes, turning. Let cool, then, using a sharp kitchen knife, remove the kernels from the cobs. In a large bowl, combine the corn, tomatoes, onion, jalapeño, cilantro (if using), and lime juice. Season to taste with salt and black pepper.

TO PAN-SEAR THE SALMON: Heat a heavy skillet for 3 minutes over high heat. Sprinkle the salmon with salt and pepper. Add the oil to the pan and coat it evenly. When the oil shimmers but does not burn, add the fillets skin-side down. Reduce heat to medium-high and cook until the skin side is well browned and the bottom halves of the fillets turn opaque, about 4 minutes. Turn and cook until the fillets are firm but not hard, 3½ minutes for medium. Turn the salmon over again and sear briefly. Remove the fillets from the pan. Let stand for 1 minute, then serve with the roasted corn salsa.

SERVES 6

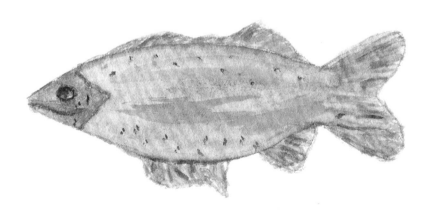

Starry Night Steamed Lobster

Starry Night Steamed Lobster
with Lemon Wedges and Melted Butter

Steamers and Crisp Garlic Bread (see page 49) are the perfect starter for this meal, which is a Hamptons classic.

Salt

2 live lobsters, about 2 pounds each

Lemon wedges

Salted butter, melted

Bring 4 to 5 quarts of water to a boil in a large pot. Add salt to taste. Add the lobsters, head first, and cover until the water boils again. Uncover and cook over high heat for about 15 minutes. The lobsters will turn pink.

Remove the lobsters from the pot and drain well. Let cool slightly. Cut in half and serve with lemon wedges and melted butter. Shell the lobsters if desired.

SERVES 2

Saffron Risotto with Shrimp and Clams

5 cups fish or vegetable stock

12 littleneck clams, scrubbed

12 ounces medium shrimp, peeled and deveined, cut into thirds, shells reserved

¼ cup extra-virgin olive oil

2 shallots, minced

2 cloves garlic, minced

Pinch of crumbled saffron threads

1 cup Arborio rice

½ cup dry white wine

6 to 8 tablespoons (up to 1 stick) unsalted butter

¼ cup chopped fresh flat-leaf parsley

Salt and freshly ground black pepper

In a large saucepan, bring the stock to a boil, then lower the heat to a simmer. Add the clams, cover, and cook until the clams open, 5 to 10 minutes. Using a slotted spoon, transfer the clams to a bowl and discard any unopened ones. Remove the clams from the shells and chop the meat.

Return the stock to a simmer and add the shrimp and clam shells. Cover and simmer for 15 minutes. Using the slotted spoon, remove the shrimp to a bowl. Pour the stock through a fine-mesh sieve over a clean saucepan to remove any grit. Return to a simmer over medium heat.

Heat the oil in another saucepan over medium heat and add the shallots and garlic. Add the saffron and cook, stirring, until the shallots are translucent, about 5 minutes. Add the rice and "toast" it for 2 minutes, stirring constantly. Add the wine and cook, stirring, until it is absorbed. Add the stock a little at a time, making sure each addition is absorbed before adding the next. Cook and add stock (you may not use it all) until the rice is al dente, 20 to 25 minutes.

Add the shrimp and cook to heat through. Remove from heat and add the butter, clams, and parsley. Season with salt and pepper to taste. Cover and let rest for a few minutes before serving.

SERVES 4 TO 6

Vegetarian Lasagna Corral

FOR THE BÉCHAMEL SAUCE

1 onion, chopped

5 cloves garlic, chopped

⅓ cup vegetable oil

3 tablespoons unbleached all-purpose flour

2 cups low-fat milk

1 cup grated Parmesan cheese

½ cup shredded Gruyère or cheddar cheese

FOR THE VEGETABLES

2 cups mushrooms, chopped

1 cup shelled peas, blanched

1 cup chopped asparagus

1 cup corn kernels

1 cup seeded and chopped red bell peppers

1 cup seeded and chopped yellow bell peppers

1 cup chopped yellow squash

2 cups chopped eggplant, peeled

3 tablespoons vegetable oil

Salt and freshly ground black pepper

Paprika

ASSEMBLY

1 pound dried lasagna noodles

1½ cups shredded mozzarella cheese

1 cup grated Parmesan cheese

Carrots, yellow squash, eggplant, and zucchini, shaved into thin ribbons to wrap around each lasagna

2½ cups tomato sauce (page 116)

Preheat the oven to 400°F.

TO MAKE THE BÉCHAMEL SAUCE: In a medium saucepan, sauté the onion and garlic in one-fourth cup of the oil until soft and translucent. Stir in the flour, then add the milk and Parmesan, and finally the Gruyère. The sauce should be thick, not runny.

TO MAKE THE VEGETABLES: In a large sauté pan, sauté the mushrooms, peas, asparagus, corn, bell peppers, squash, and eggplant together in the oil. Season with salt, pepper, and a dash of paprika.

While you are making the sauce and the vegetables, bring a pot of water to a boil and cook the lasagna noodles until they are just tender but still firm. Layer the pasta, vegetables, and sauce in a 9-by-13-inch baking dish. Top with the mozzarella and Parmesan cheeses. Bake for 40 minutes. Allow the lasagna to cool to room temperature.

While the lasagna is cooling, blanch the carrot, yellow squash, eggplant and zucchini ribbons. When the lasagna has cooled completely use 4-inch biscuit cutters to make each portion round. Put in a baking dish, top with tomato sauce, and reheat in the oven just before serving. Wrap each portion with zucchini ribbons.

SERVES 6

Stuffed Cabbage with Tomato Sauce

An individual quiche can be a delightful start to this meal.

1 (28-ounce) can diced
or whole peeled tomatoes

1 small onion, chopped

1 tablespoon vegetable oil

3 tablespoons lemon juice

1½ pounds button mushrooms,
stems trimmed, chopped

½ cup panko bread crumbs

2 cups cooked brown rice

2 eggs

Salt and freshly ground
black pepper

1 medium head green
cabbage, cored

In a mixing bowl, crush the tomatoes until the pieces have broken down to a pulp.

In a large saucepan, heat the onion and oil over low heat. Add the tomatoes and lemon juice and simmer, covered, for 10 minutes.

Put the mushrooms in a food processor and pulse until they have broken down to a chunky pulp. Pour into a mixing bowl and add the bread crumbs, rice, eggs, and a pinch of salt and pepper. Cover the bowl.

Preheat the oven to 375°F. Bring a large pot of salted water to a boil. Add the cabbage and let it boil for 1 minute. Remove the cabbage with tongs and tear off at least 8 large leaves to use for stuffing. Cut out and discard the tough middle stem of each leaf. Place a 1-inch-long log of mushroom mixture inside each leaf and wrap, tucking in the end pieces as you go. Slice the rest of the cabbage into ½-inch pieces and place in a covered casserole or Dutch oven. Place the stuffed cabbage rolls on top of the shredded cabbage. Top with the tomato sauce and cover.

Bake, covered, for 1½ hours. Remove from heat and let rest for 10 minutes before serving.

SERVES 4 TO 6

Desserts

Andrew & Ricky's Chocolate Mousse
Flourless Chocolate Cake

Andrew & Ricky's Chocolate Mousse

When Andrew was a little boy, he loved to help me make chocolate mousse. After patiently sitting on the counter watching the procedure, he would stand up high on the kitchen stool and run his little fingers all over the inside of the mixing bowl and then lick them clean. And he especially loved the part when he got to lick the big wooden spoon.

8 ounces semisweet chocolate

3 free-range organic eggs, separated

2 tablespoons rum

2 tablespoons sugar

¼ cup heavy cream

Melt the chocolate in the top of a double boiler over simmering water. Add the egg yolks and rum. Beat the egg whites until frothy. Gradually add the sugar. Beat until stiff peaks form. Gently fold into the chocolate mixture. Whip the cream and gently fold it into the chocolate mixture.

Refrigerate until ready to serve.

SERVES 4 TO 6

Flourless Chocolate Cake

The family always gathers together for the holidays. This cake works well for us at Passover.

Nonstick cooking spray

1 pound (4 sticks) butter

1 pound semisweet chocolate

2 cups sugar

8 eggs

Preheat the oven to 325°F.

Line the bottom of a 9-inch springform pan with parchment paper and spray the entire surface, bottom, and sides with nonstick spray. Wrap the outside of the pan with tin foil so that the water bath cannot enter.

Melt the butter and chocolate in the top of a double boiler over simmering water. Whisk in the sugar and eggs. The batter will separate, so beat until it is well mixed.

Pour the batter into the prepared pan and set it into a larger pan. Pour hot water into a larger pan until it's halfway up the sides of the springform pan. Bake uncovered in a water bath for 70 minutes. Remove from water to cool.

Refrigerate overnight to allow the cake to set.

SERVES 8 TO 10

(Clockwise from top left): *Moby-Dick* by James Edwin McConnell. A portrait of James Fenimore Cooper by Alonzo Chappel. Termagant from *Last of the Mohicans* by Newell Convers Wyeth, ca. 1919. A frontispiece of *Moby-Dick* by Mead Schaeffer. Portrait of Colonel Alden Spooner by Hubbard Latham Fordham, ca. 1832. An illustration of *Uncle Tom's Cabin* from the Courier Litho. Co., of Buffalo, N.Y., ca. 1899. Frontispiece of *The Last of the Mohicans* from 1949 by American School. *Ann and Eliza Dusenberry* by Orlando Hand Bears, ca. 1838.

THE LAST OF THE MOHICANS

J. FENIMORE COOPER

MOBY DICK
OR
THE WHITE WHALE

BY
HERMAN MELVILLE

ILLUSTRATED BY
MEAD SCHAEFFER

NEW YORK
DODD, MEAD AND COMPANY
MCMXXIII

UNCLE TOM'S CABIN

Creativity Flourishes in the Hamptons

The beauty of the landscape and the quality of the ever-changing light of the Hamptons have been a source of inspiration for the works of many artists, architects, and authors. A great chapter in the history of American art, architecture, and literature was written on these shores.

In the early days of the settlement of East Hampton, Lion Gardiner, New York State's first English settler, offered the use of his personal library to attract the preacher Thomas James to the area. The Indians as well as the townsfolk benefited from his literary interests and his sermons. Gardiner and James learned the Montaukett language. Gardiner wrote one of the earliest accounts of Indian lore, and James translated parts of the English Bible, including the Catechism, into the Indian language. After forty-six years of service, James was succeeded by Nathaniel Hunting, a Harvard theology-degree graduate educated by Increase Mather and his son, Cotton. Succeeding Hunting was the town's third minister, Samuel Buell. Next came the pastor Lyman Beecher, whose powerful sermon "The Remedy for Dueling" was written in response to the duel of 1804 in which Alexander Hamilton was shot and killed by Vice President Aaron Burr. Beecher had thirteen children, some of whom became famous in their own right: Catherine Beecher, an advocate of education for women; Henry Ward Beecher, the orator and abolitionist preacher; and Harriet Beecher Stowe, author of *Uncle Tom's Cabin*.

In 1819 James Fenimore Cooper[1] came to Sag Harbor intending to start a whaling business there, but became disenchanted with the enterprise. Instead, he took up his wife's challenge when she suggested that he try his hand at writing. Thereafter he wrote many popular stories, including *The Leatherstocking Tales*, a series of five novels that depicted the clashes between Indians and settlers on the frontier. One of his best-known books, considered by many to be a masterpiece, is his novel *The Last of the Mohicans* (1826). Several of his novels had nautical themes and took place in Montauk and the Sag Harbor area. Another great writer, Herman Melville,[2] in his epic novel *Moby-Dick* (1851), depicted whaling and captured the excitement of the chase. Though written in Massachusetts and New York City, his classic sea tales trace their genesis to the East End of Long Island.

At the height of the whaling industry, new homes were built in the towns. In Sag Harbor, fine goods were in great demand to outfit the buildings. Portraiture was popular, and the local gentry became immortalized by the artist Hubbard Latham Fordham and later by his distant cousin Orlando Hand Bears. The former's style was somewhat awkward and naive, and the latter's was softer and more personal. Bears's landscape of circa 1835 may have been the first professional one of the region. From portraiture, artists were turning their attention to the land and especially to the coastline.

---

[1] James Fenimore Cooper: author of *Precaution* (1820), *The Spy* (1821), *The Pioneers* (1823), *The Sea Lions* (1849), *Miles Wallingford* (1844), and *Jack Tier* (1848).
[2] Herman Melville: *Typee: A Peep at Polynesian Life* (1846), *Omoo: A Narrative of Adventures in the South Seas* (1847), *Mardi: And a Voyage Thither* (1849), *Redburn: His First Voyage* (1849), *White-Jacket, or The World in a Man-of-War* (1850), *Moby-Dick: or, The Whale* (1851), *Pierre: or, The Ambiguities* (1852), *Isle of the Cross* (1853), *Israel Potter: His Fifty Years of Exile* (1855), *The Confidence-Man: His Masquerade* (1857), and *Billy Budd, Sailor (An Inside Narrative)* (1924, published posthumously).

William Cullen Bryant in 1874 wrote poetry describing the "peculiar charm of the sandy landscape that stretched eastward from Southampton to Montauk." Walt Whitman wrote "From Montauk Points," which included these lines:

> I stand as on some mighty eagle's beak,
> Eastward the sea absorbing, viewing,
>   (nothing but sea and sky,)
> The tossing waves, the foam, the ships in
>   the distance,
> The wild unrest, the snowy, curling
>   caps—that inbound urge and urge
>   of waves,
> Seeking the shores forever.

It would later appear in the 1888 edition of *Leaves of Grass*, his short self-published book of twelve poems. Whitman created epic poetry about the sea, fishermen, and farmers. East Hampton had its own resident novelist, Cornelia Huntingdon, who descriptively captured the lifestyle and the beauty of the region in her novel *Sea-spray: A Long Island Village*.

In 1876, at one hundred years old, our young nation was proud of its pioneer spirit. Artists focused on the American landscape. New York City was the cultural center of America. The proximity and convenience of the Hamptons provided an as-yet-untapped subject matter that the artists could explore.

The Tile Club, founded in 1877, was an informal association of professional artists, writers, and architects who met regularly to exchange ideas, paint ceramic tiles, and organize summer drawing expeditions. As decorative art was becoming a popular trend in America, they met at one another's studios to decorate Spanish ceramic tiles and devise ways to market their work. Among the club's

members were the landscape artists Winslow Homer, William Merrit Chase, Robert Swain Gifford, and Edwin Austin Abbey; the sculptor Augustus Saint-Gaudens; and the architect Stanford White.

In 1878 eleven members of the club boarded a train to Babylon, sailed in a sloop, rode in a stagecoach, and then boarded another train, finally disembarking in Bridgehampton. They stopped to sketch the local windmill and the surrounding area. They went on to East Hampton, settling into boardinghouses. Enchanted by the endless scenery of ocean on the horizon, dunes, bays, and marshes, they rendered the gulls reeling overhead, sun glinting across the ocean, crashing waves, and fishing and sailing vessels in the distance. They painted the charming villages, farms, and life of rustic simplicity. The artists continued on to Montauk by carriage, and as they left the flatlands they mounted the Montauk hills, which offered breathtaking views of the wild ocean scenery. They painted the old colonial houses, barns, windmills, beaches, sea, magnificent precipices, and the lighthouse. The subject matter and the glorious light both thrilled and inspired them.

In February 1879 an account of their sojourn along with accompanying drawings appeared in *Scribner's Monthly* magazine. Southampton, Bridgehampton, East Hampton, Sag Harbor, Amagansett, and even the far reaches of Montauk became the artists' haven, attracting both landscape and genre painters. The area became known as the "American Barbizon,"[3] a true artists' colony where portable easels, folding chairs, and umbrellas dotted the fields, farmyards, and beaches. The primitive and picturesque gold mine had been discovered, luring artists and authors—and

[3]Barbizon is a village near the Forest of Fontainebleau in France. From 1830 to 1870, when the weather turned warmer, landscape and naturalist artists from Paris traveled out of the city to work in and from nature, painting *en plein air*. Barbizon was a particularly popular place for them to visit.

soon a deluge of tourists—to fill the boarding-houses and summer rentals to capacity.

By the late nineteenth century, as the railroad was passing through the villages all the way to Montauk Point, farmland began to be divided into large plots. Some acreage was sold to individuals. Grand yet informal sprawling mansions of shingle style were comfortably integrated with the colonial architecture of the villages.

In 1879 a New York businessman, Arthur Benson, paid $151,000 for a large plot of land from Napeague all the way to Montauk Point to establish the Montauk Association, which he envisioned would become an exclusive community for sport and fishing. Stanford White of the architectural firm McKim, Mead and White was commissioned to design the buildings, a grouping of seven houses built in 1880 above the bluffs of Montauk Point. (Years later they became known as the Seven Sisters.) Positioned in a V formation, the houses took advantage of the sea breezes and the uninterrupted ocean view. Frederick Law Olmsted (who also designed Central Park) did the landscaping.

The novelist, translator, and critic Charles de Kay, famous in the New York social scene, called the new arrivals to East Hampton circa 1883 "invaders" and wrote that their expensive country homes would contaminate its picturesque charm and restful quietude. He wrote about the area lovingly and wished to protect it. Perhaps, in fact, it was the writers and the artists themselves who were innocently complicit in advertising and exposing the area. No longer a quiet resort, the Hamptons were becoming a recreational destination for many.

(Clockwise from top left): Robert Swain Gifford's *Seconnet Rock, New Bedford, Massachusetts*, ca. 1865. The Moran house in East Hampton. *Rowing Home* by Winslow Homer, ca. 1890. *Morning at the Breakwater, Shinnecock* by William Merritt Chase, ca. 1897. *May Day Morning* by Edwin Austin Abbey, ca. 1890–1894. *Summer Squall* by Winslow Homer, ca. 1904. *East Hampton, Long Island, Sand Dunes* by Thomas Moran, ca. 1892. An illustration of the Tile Club from *Scribner's Monthly* entitled Sketching at East Hampton. The cover page of *Scribner's Monthly* from February, 1879.

Thomas Moran, the landscape painter known for his dramatic panoramas of Yellowstone, and his wife, Mary Nimmo, an etcher of renown, fell in love with this simpler, more pastoral area. After renting rooms for a few summers, they had a local builder construct the first studio-residence in East Hampton on Main Street in 1884. Moran was the first artist to make East Hampton his permanent summer home, and the house—an eccentric experiment designed by Moran himself with painted gables, odd chimneys, and arched dormer windows—became the place for social gatherings and entertainment. Moran's family included sixteen painters, printmakers, and illustrators, who enjoyed the use of "The Studio," and it became known as an East Hampton artists' colony.

In 1891 the American impressionist William Merrit Chase became the director of the Shinnecock Summer School of Art in Southampton. He taught his students how to look at nature with a fresh eye and work spontaneously *en plein air* (outdoors), finishing canvases on the spot rather than sketching first and completing the paintings in the studio. He taught them the joy of painting, telling them to be happy and sing as they worked. Many of his students, like Charles Demuth, Marsden Hartley, and Georgia O'Keeffe, became notable American artists in their own right.

The school was based on a utopian compound called "The Art Village," with shingled cottages that were precious, picturesque, and toylike. The architect Stanford White was a friend of Chase, and both were members of the Tile Club. White designed and built Chase's studio-residence for him and his family. Chase's artistic perspective illuminated the aesthetic value of the Shinnecock

Hills of Southampton. His work brought attention to the area and property values soared hundredfold.

A wealthy New York lawyer and backer of Chase, Samuel Parrish, had the first museum in the area built in Southampton in 1897 to house his Italian Renaissance collection. Meanwhile, East Hampton grew as a fashionable resort as well, as a place for artists to congregate and form a colony. Many of its well-to-do residents happened also to be budding artists.

The American impressionist painter Frederick Childe Hassam bought a cottage in East Hampton in 1919 after first visiting the area and falling under its spell in 1898. Many of his paintings, drawings, and etchings depict local subjects, landmarks, and landscaping. He rendered the town's stately elms and English-style smock windmills, and often painted scenes of the Maidstone Club, a private country and sports club established in 1891 on the oceanfront.

Albert and Adele Herter were artists and children of socialites and dubbed "The Quintessential East Hampton couple of this period," by *Studios by the Sea*. As a wedding gift from Albert's mother, the couple was given seventy-five acres on Georgica Pond in East Hampton, where they built a huge Mediterranean villa designed by the architect Grosvenor Atterbury in 1899. The home contained his-and-hers studios to accommodate his penchant for art and decoration and hers for landscape architecture and portrait painting. The estate, known as "The Creeks" because it was bordered by two creeks, has subsequently had many prominent owners.

By the early 1900s, new homes were being constructed in all of the picturesque locations that the artists had chosen as inspirations for their paintings. These homes expressed freedom from restricted city life, and ranged from sprawling and romantic to English classical. These houses were grander than their shingle-style forerunners.

In the 1920s Carl Graham Fisher, the real-estate developer who had created the Indianapolis Speedway and Miami Beach, the most successful American resort to date, studied the Montauk coastline, its rocky shore and rolling hills, and purchased ten thousand acres. Development began immediately. Roads and pipelines were laid, land was cleared, and new buildings went up. He also built an eighteen-hole golf course, a polo field, a beach club, a yacht club, a railroad station, and an office building. He commissioned the architects of the Waldorf Astoria to build a hotel. However, the unpredictable weather and the short season were not conducive to maintaining a consistent business. The stock market crash of 1929 also helped to put an end to this endeavor.

During the Depression, tourism, agriculture, and the fishing industries suffered, but wealthy people continued to summer in the Hamptons. In 1931 some members of the Maidstone Club—including the Herters,

Childe Hassam, Maude Jewett, Hamilton King, Francis Newton, and Mr. and Mrs. Lorenzo E. Woodhouse—joined together to build the "Guild Hall" of East Hampton, with the intention of creating a cultural center with a theater and art gallery. The theater was dedicated to John Drew, and the main gallery was dedicated by Childe Hassam to Thomas Moran, who was credited as the founder of East Hampton as an artists' retreat. Work from Tile Club members and their contemporaries was displayed at the first exhibition as a tribute, acknowledging their part in "discovering" East Hampton.

On September 21, 1938, the Great New England Hurricane hit the entire northeastern seaboard, leaving more than six hundred dead and seven hundred injured. It damaged or destroyed more than fifty thousand homes and farms. The east coast of Long Island, especially the Hamptons, suffered a severe blow. Montauk came close to losing its entire fishing industry.

Less than a year later, German troops swarmed into Poland, and war was declared in Europe.

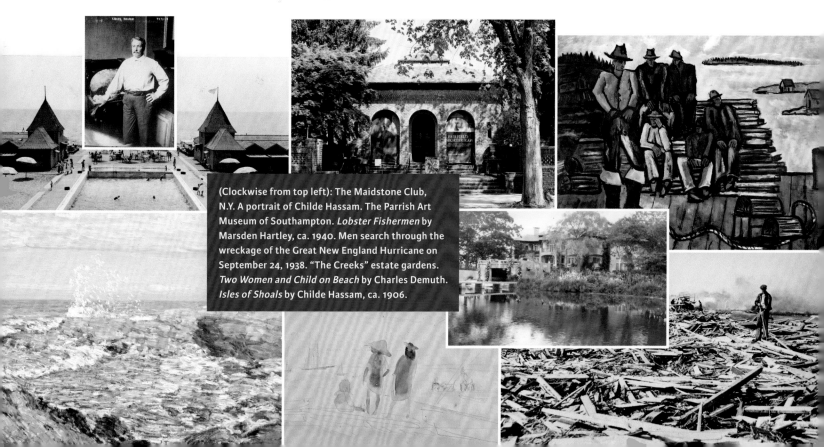

(Clockwise from top left): The Maidstone Club, N.Y. A portrait of Childe Hassam. The Parrish Art Museum of Southampton. *Lobster Fishermen* by Marsden Hartley, ca. 1940. Men search through the wreckage of the Great New England Hurricane on September 24, 1938. "The Creeks" estate gardens. *Two Women and Child on Beach* by Charles Demuth. *Isles of Shoals* by Childe Hassam, ca. 1906.

CHAPTER 2

Amagansett

W e lived in two homes in Amagansett. The first house was a very modern triangular A-frame set on a road in the midst of a cluster of other homes. On the second floor it had a large, high-ceilinged living room facing the road. The kitchen floated in this space, and the bedrooms were located in the rear. The entrance was on the lower level, which had another bedroom, a recreation room, and a laundry room.

The second house was a glass-walled high-tech box set opposite the beach at the end of a long road. It had a rectangular deck on the second floor, where we ate most of our meals, weather permitting. We had a skylight in our bedroom. From our bed we could watch the shooting stars that appeared in the dark, star-studded sky that signaled the end of August. Both houses were built directly on the sand dunes, with beach grass and scrubby black pines for landscaping.

Andrew and David, Amagansett, August 1973.

It seems that the only shaped house we missed was a revolving sphere. At this point, Ralph and I had two wonderful young sons: Andrew, who by now was four years old, and David, his younger brother, who was not yet two.

In those days, the roads in Amagansett consisted of earth, sand, and pebbles, firm enough for bike riding and baby-carriage pushing, and soft and cool enough for traveling barefoot to and from the beach. Keeping the roads this way served to slow down the car traffic. This allowed for many uninterrupted softball games and for all the children to play safely in front of their homes in a communal environment.

I remember the balmy summer evenings, when the sun stayed out way after the neighborhood children had had their baths and dinners after a long day at the beach. Playtimes, which included ball games and riding toys, continued until dark. No one needed a television, and the children and their parents were exhausted and content to rest at the end of a long and active day.

I spent my days at the beach in Amagansett while Ralph worked in the city during the week and joined us on the weekends. I cared for the boys all day long, and after their bedtime I would put order to the home, prepare simple menus and grocery lists, and read myself to sleep. These were the days of quick meals focused around the children and a very casual beach atmosphere.

Ralph and the boys, August 1972.

Breakfasts

Bagels and Flagels with Whipped Vegetable
and Chive Cream Cheese, Strawberry Cream
Cheese, or Smoked Salmon and Cream Cheese

Poached Egg on Toasted Seven-Grain Bread

Banana-Blueberry Whole Wheat Pancakes
with Blueberry Syrup

Bagels and Flagels

with Whipped Vegetable and Chive Cream Cheese, Strawberry Cream Cheese, or Smoked Salmon and Cream Cheese

When my children were little, they loved bagels for lunch. I would toast them and slather them with peanut butter and jelly, or pile them high with tuna fish or egg salad. Today there is a variation on the bagel. I had never heard of a "flagel" until a few years ago. A flagel is a large flattened bagel, often completely coated in the various usual bagel toppings. I highly recommend that you try one of these new Hamptons favorites with your choice of "schmear"!

Poached Egg

on Toasted Seven-Grain Bread

I never liked poached eggs cooked in a form. To me, the whites of the eggs get too hard when they are prepared that way. I like them to be cooked right in the water. The trick is to add a drop of white vinegar to the simmering water. Crack each shell separately, and slip its contents into a small bowl. From the bowl, slip the raw egg gently into the simmering water, trying not to disturb the egg too much. Let the egg simmer, but never allow the water to come to a full rolling boil. Once the egg is cooked, scoop it out of the water with a slotted spoon and place it on top of a crispy triangle of multigrain toast. I like to grind fresh black pepper on my poached eggs.

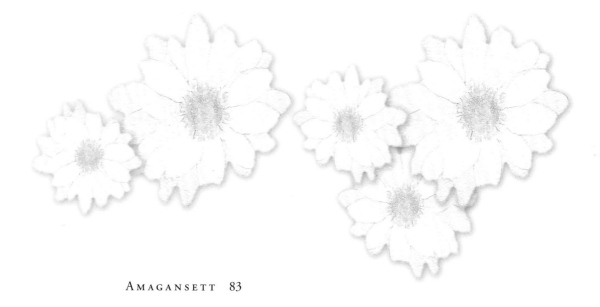

Banana-Blueberry Whole Wheat Pancakes

When the children went to day camp in the summertime, we had our own little breakfast factory going in the morning. Everyone had a job. For this meal I would make the batter, then mash the bananas into it and drop blueberries on top of the pancakes as they fried on the hot griddle. One child would set the table, one would pour the milk, and one would stand on a stool at the kitchen counter and make freshly squeezed orange juice. After breakfast, we all cleared the table together and raced out to meet the camp bus.

2 cups buttermilk

3 large eggs

1 medium-size ripe banana, mashed

6 tablespoons (¾ stick) unsalted butter, melted and cooled, plus additional for the pan

¾ cup all-purpose flour

½ cup whole wheat flour

¼ cup wheat germ

1 teaspoon salt

2 teaspoons baking powder

1½ teaspoons baking soda

3 tablespoons granulated sugar

2 cups blueberries

Preheat the oven to 200°F.

Whisk the buttermilk, eggs, mashed banana, and butter in a mixing bowl. Mix the dry ingredients together in a separate bowl. Add the buttermilk mixture to the dry ingredients and whisk until combined.

Heat a griddle and brush it with butter. Pour the batter onto the griddle by ⅓-cup measures, then sprinkle each pancake with 2 tablespoons of blueberries and cook until bubbly, flip over, and cook until golden on the bottom.

Keep warm in the oven until ready to serve. Serve with syrup and fresh berries on the side.

SERVES 4 TO 6

Blueberry Syrup

6 cups blueberries

3 cups sugar

Zest of 1 lemon

3 cups water

¼ cup fresh lemon juice, or to taste

Combine the blueberries and 1½ cups of water. Bring the mixture to a boil and simmer, covered, for 10 minutes. Puree the mixture through a sieve into a bowl. Discard the solids.

Combine the sugar, lemon zest, and 3 cups of water. Bring to a boil. Stir until the sugar dissolves and boil to 220° (test with a candy thermometer).

Strain and discard the zest, add the blueberry mixture and boil the syrup, stirring, for 1 minute. Cool, skim off the froth, and stir in the lemon juice.

Pour the syrup into glass jars with tight-fitting lids. It will keep for about 3 months, refrigerated. Serve warm over pancakes.

MAKES ABOUT 6 CUPS

Luncheon

Bill's Crispy Pizza with Spinach and Peppers

Coast Guard Curried Shrimp Salad

Potato, Cheese, and Fruit Blintzes
Served with a Dollop of Sour Cream

Cold Borscht Served with a Dollop
of Sour Cream

East End Tuna Croquettes
Served with a Summer Fruit Salad

Bill's Crispy Pizza with Spinach and Peppers

FOR THE DOUGH

1 (¼-ounce) envelope active dry yeast

1 cup very warm water

3½ cups all-purpose flour

1 teaspoon salt

2 tablespoons olive oil, plus more for coating the dough

FOR THE PIZZA

Cornmeal

1 cup homemade tomato sauce (see page 116)

1 cup chopped spinach, cooked and squeezed dry

1 cup red bell pepper, cut into 2-inch-long julienne strips

1 cup grated mozzarella cheese

TO MAKE THE DOUGH: In a small bowl, stir the yeast and water together and let stand until the yeast granules dissolve and bubble, about 10 minutes.

Combine the flour and salt in a large bowl. Make a well in the center and add the oil and the yeast mixture. Stir well until a dough forms. Transfer the dough to a floured surface and knead it for 10 minutes. Lightly coat the dough with oil and leave at room temperature to rise until doubled in size, 1 to 2 hours.

TO MAKE THE PIZZA: Preheat the oven to 500°F.

Roll out the dough on a floured surface into a 14-inch circle. Sprinkle a baking sheet with a thin coating of cornmeal and place the rolled-out dough on top. Spread a thin layer of the sauce over the dough. Arrange the spinach and pepper on top. Sprinkle with the mozzarella. Bake until the cheese is melted and the dough is cooked through, 10 to 15 minutes. Slice and serve hot.

SERVES 4 TO 6

Coast Guard Curried Shrimp Salad

¼ cup light mayonnaise

2 tablespoons low-fat yogurt

1 teaspoon curry powder

½ teaspoon grated lemon zest

1 tablespoon fresh lemon juice

¼ teaspoon salt

1 rib celery, finely chopped

½ cup seedless grapes, halved

1 pound cooked shrimp

Lettuce

In a large bowl, stir together the mayonnaise, yogurt, curry powder, lemon zest, lemon juice, and salt. Add the celery, grapes, and shrimp and mix well. Serve on a bed of lettuce.

SERVES 4

Potato, Cheese, and Fruit Blintzes
and Cold Borscht

Potato, Cheese, and Fruit Blintzes
Served with a Dollop of Sour Cream

A blintz is a crepe filled with either a sweet cheese-based or savory potato-onion mixture. The delicate pancake is wrapped around the stuffing and secured at both ends so the filling remains within. Blintzes can be served for breakfast or lunch, or as a side dish or dessert, depending upon their fillings. I like to serve potato blintzes with some fresh sour cream on the side. Sweet blintzes are nice with a ladleful of fruit compote on top, as well as an optional dollop of fresh sour cream. Whichever is your favorite, they are homey and delicious.

FOR THE POTATO FILLING

4 medium potatoes, peeled and cooked

2 onions, chopped and sautéed

1 large egg, lightly beaten

Salt and pepper to taste

FOR THE CHEESE FILLING

1¼ cups cottage cheese

2 tablespoons cream cheese

1 large egg

1½ tablespoons sugar

1 teaspoon vanilla extract

Grated zest of 1 orange

FOR THE FRUIT COMPOTE

2 cups blueberries or pitted cherries

Juice of ½ lemon

2 tablespoons sugar

Pinch of ground cinnamon

FOR THE SWEET CREPES

1 cup all-purpose flour

1 cup whole milk

3 large eggs

1 teaspoon vanilla extract

2 teaspoons sugar

Pinch of salt

2 tablespoons unsalted butter, melted

Sour cream

TO MAKE THE POTATO FILLING: Blend all the ingredients together in a food processor until smooth. Add salt and pepper to taste.

TO MAKE THE CHEESE FILLING: Blend all the ingredients together in a food processor until smooth. Set aside until ready to fill the pancakes.

TO MAKE THE FRUIT COMPOTE: Combine 1 cup of the fruit and the remaining ingredients together in a small saucepan. Bring to a boil, stirring until the berries burst and the mixture takes on the consistency of jam. Add the remaining fruit and cook for 1 minute. Transfer to ramekins for serving alongside the cheese blintzes.

TO MAKE THE SWEET CREPES: In a large bowl, combine the flour, milk, eggs, vanilla, sugar, and salt. Whisk until smooth. The batter can be stored, refrigerated, overnight.

Lightly coat a 9-inch crepe pan or heavy skillet with butter. Heat over medium-high heat until almost smoking. Ladle ½ cup of the batter into the skillet and tilt in all directions to spread the batter evenly. Cook until the underside is set. Flip over and cook the other side for an additional 2 to 3 minutes. Transfer to a plate and keep warm. Repeat with the remaining batter to make 10 crepes.

Place a crepe on a work surface and spoon 3 to 4 table-spoons of potato or cheese filling into the center. Fold in the sides and roll the crepe away from you. Set aside, seam-side down, until all the crepes have been filled. At this point, they may be covered and refrigerated for up to 24 hours.

Heat 1 tablespoon of the butter in a large sauté pan and add about half of the blintzes. Cook until golden brown on the bottom and the filling is heated through, about 3 minutes. Turn and cook the other side until golden brown, about 2 more minutes. Remove from heat and keep warm; repeat with the remaining blintzes. Serve immediately with sour cream and the fruit compote.

SERVES 10

Cold Borscht
Served with a Dollop of Sour Cream

2 quarts water

6 medium beets, peeled and grated

1 large onion, chopped

1 cup canned chopped tomatoes

Salt and freshly ground black pepper

2 large eggs

Sour cream

Fresh chives

Bring the water, beets, and onion to a boil in a pot and simmer for 45 minutes. Add the tomatoes and salt and pepper to taste, and continue cooking for another 45 minutes.

Reserve 1 cup of the beets and liquid. Puree the remaining soup in a blender in small batches. Return the pureed soup to the pot.

In a medium bowl, beat the eggs and gradually add the reserved beet mixture. Stir the egg mixture into the soup and bring to a boil one more time, then remove from heat. Chill in the refrigerator. Serve cold. Garnish each serving with 1 tablespoon sour cream and a sprinkle of chives.

SERVES 6

East End Tuna Croquettes
Served with Summer Fruit Salad

When Andrew, David, and Dylan were growing up, they were not the best fish eaters in the world. I would serve them homemade tuna croquettes with tartar sauce and applesauce on the side. This seemed to work, since the fish was disguised!

2 (6-ounce) cans of albacore tuna, drained and mashed

2 scallions, chopped

¼ cup all-purpose flour

2 eggs, beaten

1 cup panko bread crumbs

Salt and pepper to taste

Safflower oil (for frying)

Combine the tuna and scallions. Shape the mixture into small patties.

Put the flour, eggs, and bread crumbs in three separate shallow bowls. Dip each patty into the flour, then the eggs. Coat with the bread crumbs. Heat the oil in a skillet. Fry the patties until golden brown, 2 minutes on each side.

Cool for a few minutes, then serve with Tartar Sauce (see page 110).

SERVES 4

First Courses
Mushroom Soup

Cold Asparagus with Vinaigrette

Spring Pea Soup

Parmesan Crisps

Chilled Carrot Soup with Dilled Orzo

Gazpacho

Mushroom Soup

I have included a number of my favorite soups in this book. Most of them are not only delicious but colorful and visually attractive. Not so with this mushroom soup. However, it is so flavorful that I must include it here. It is one of my family's favorite soups for all seasons.

¼ cup olive oil

1 onion, chopped

2 cloves garlic, chopped

2 cups cremini mushrooms, sliced

1 cup shiitake mushrooms, sliced

1 cup button mushrooms, sliced

2 tablespoons all-purpose flour

1½ cups vegetable broth

1½ cups low-fat milk

2 sprigs fresh thyme

2 tablespoons chopped fresh parsley

1 tablespoon sherry

Salt and freshly ground black pepper

In a saucepan, heat the oil over medium heat, then add the onion and garlic and sauté until soft, about 4 minutes. Add the mushrooms and cook for 5 minutes. Sprinkle in the flour and mix well.

Pour in the broth and milk, and add the thyme. Bring to a boil, then lower the heat and simmer for about 10 minutes.

Remove the thyme sprigs, then puree the soup using an immersion blender, food processor, or blender. Add the parsley, sherry, and salt and pepper to taste. Serve hot.

SERVES 6

Cold Asparagus with Vinaigrette

1 pound asparagus, tough ends trimmed

1 tablespoon fresh lemon juice

3 tablespoons white wine vinegar

2 small shallots, finely chopped

1 clove garlic, minced

1 teaspoon Dijon mustard

2 teaspoons honey

¼ cup grape-seed oil

¼ cup extra-virgin olive oil

Salt and freshly ground black pepper

Steam the asparagus until tender, approximately 4 minutes. Immediately put it in ice water to stop the cooking. Drain and keep chilled in the refrigerator.

In a small bowl, whisk together the lemon juice, vinegar, shallots, garlic, mustard, and honey until combined. Slowly pour in the oils and whisk vigorously until creamy. Add salt and pepper to taste.

Lay the asparagus on a platter and drizzle with the vinaigrette, or serve it on the side.

SERVES 6

Spring Pea Soup

My son David loves soup. He will ask, "What kind of soup do you have?" rather than "What are we having for dinner?" We both enjoy this bright green spring pea soup to start, or as an accompaniment to a summer meal.

I love the addition of the Goat Cheese Soufflé (see page 39) afloat and the Parmesan Crisps on the side to provide a variety of taste, texture, and color. The result is a simple soup turned into an elegant, attractive one, especially with the magical additions. When serving this for dinner with a soufflé, I serve it hot, but it's also delicious as a cold soup at lunchtime.

¼ cup (½ stick) unsalted butter

1 medium onion, chopped

2 cloves garlic, minced

3¾ cups chicken or vegetable stock

1 pound fresh peas, shelled, or 4 cups frozen peas

Salt and freshly ground black pepper

1 teaspoon chopped fresh mint

Melt the butter in a saucepan and sauté the onion and garlic until translucent, 3 to 4 minutes. Add the stock and peas. Season with salt and pepper to taste. Bring to a boil. Lower the heat and simmer for 6 to 8 minutes.

Add the mint, then puree the soup in batches in a blender or by using an immersion blender. Check for seasoning. The soup can be served either hot or chilled. To serve chilled, put in the refrigerator for at least 4 hours.

SERVES 4

Parmesan Crisps

I serve these beside the soup plate. Some family members even enjoy dipping them right into the pea soup. They are incredibly easy and a savory delight.

8 ounces Parmesan cheese, finely grated

Freshly ground black pepper

Smoked paprika or ground cayenne (optional)

Preheat the oven to 350°F.

Season the cheese with the pepper and paprika or cayenne. Using a tablespoon measure, place the cheese in mounds on a baking sheet lined with a nonstick silicone pad or greased parchment paper. Flatten the mounds with the back of a spoon, keeping them at least 4 inches apart. Bake on the center rack of the oven until the cheese has melted and is lacy, 5 to 6 minutes. Work with one batch at a time to prevent overcooking. Let cool until firm, then remove from the pan.

SERVES 6

Chilled Carrot Soup with Dilled Orzo

2 tablespoons unsalted butter

1 tablespoon olive oil

1 medium onion, chopped

1 pound carrots, peeled and sliced

½ teaspoon freshly grated nutmeg

2 tablespoons honey

4 cups chicken stock

Salt

1½ cups uncooked orzo

3 tablespoons finely chopped fresh dill, plus sprigs for garnish

3 tablespoons fresh lemon juice

Heat 1 tablespoon of the butter and the oil in a large saucepan over medium heat. Add the onion and sauté until translucent, about 5 minutes. Add the carrots, nutmeg, and honey. Continue sautéing for about 10 minutes. Add the stock, cover, and simmer until the carrots are tender, about 10 minutes. Puree the soup either using an immersion blender or in batches in a blender. Let cool for 10 minutes. Refrigerate for at least 4 hours or overnight.

Bring a large pot of lightly salted water to a boil. Add the orzo and cook until al dente, 8 to 10 minutes. Drain.

Lightly stir the remaining 1 tablespoon butter into the orzo, to coat. Let cool. Gently stir in the dill and lemon juice. Refrigerate until ready to serve. Ladle the chilled soup into bowls. Place a tablespoon of orzo in the center of each serving. Serve garnished with a sprig of dill.

SERVES 6

Gazpacho

2 pounds tomatoes

1 clove garlic, minced

¼ cup minced red onion

1 cucumber, peeled and chopped

1 yellow bell pepper, seeded and chopped

1 red bell pepper, seeded and chopped

1 teaspoon sugar

1 tablespoon sherry vinegar

1 quart tomato juice

Dash of Tabasco sauce

Dash of Worcestershire sauce

Salt and freshly ground black pepper to taste

To easily peel the tomatoes, cut a small X into one end of each tomato. Drop them in a pot of boiling water for 1 to 2 minutes. Remove them from the pot with a slotted spoon and plunge into cold water. The skins will easily slip off.

Combine all the ingredients in a blender and puree until smooth. Taste and adjust the seasoning. Chill for 1 hour before serving.

SERVES 6

Chilled Carrot Soup with Dilled Orzo

Main Courses and Side Dishes

London Broil with Creamy Horseradish Sauce

Beef, Veal, and Chicken Meat Loaf

Baked White and Sweet Potato Wedges

Herb-Roasted Organic Chicken

Sweet Potato Fritters

Sunset Organic Chicken Pot Pie

Beer-Batter Fish and Chips with Homemade Tartar Sauce

Crisp Matchstick Potatoes

Grilled Swordfish Steaks

Shrimp and Scallop Burgers

Avocado and Mango Dressing

Spaghetti with Clam Sauce

Hamptons Stuffed Eggplant

Baby Shell Pasta with Fresh Tomato Sauce

Phyllo Vegetable Stack

London Broil
with Creamy Horseradish Sauce

One of the first meals that I mastered was London broil with baked potatoes and simple steamed vegetables. I made it for Ralph and the children because it was an easy, quick meal to prepare. It was a dinner they often requested, and it became a basic meal that I could count on in my gradually growing repertoire. As my confidence grew, I started to prepare it for weekend guests.

FOR THE LONDON BROIL

3 cloves garlic, minced

2 teaspoons fresh lemon juice

3 tablespoons balsamic vinegar

2 tablespoons Worcestershire sauce

¼ cup red wine

1 tablespoon soy sauce

1 teaspoon honey

Salt and freshly ground black pepper to taste

2 to 2½ pounds flank steak or top round

FOR THE CREAMY HORSERADISH SAUCE

¼ cup prepared horseradish

½ cup sour cream

1 tablespoon Dijon mustard

Dash of Worcestershire sauce

1 tablespoon cider vinegar

Salt and freshly ground black pepper to taste

1 teaspoon finely chopped fresh chives

TO MAKE THE LONDON BROIL: To make the marinade, mix together all the ingredients except the meat. Place the meat in a shallow dish and cover with the marinade. Cover with plastic wrap and refrigerate for at least 4 hours but no more than 24 hours.

Remove the meat from the refrigerator and bring it to room temperature before cooking. Preheat a grill to high, oil the grate, and set it 5 to 6 inches above the coals. (Alternatively, preheat the broiler to high and set a rack 5 to 6 inches below the heat source.)

Remove the meat from the marinade (discard the marinade) and pat it dry with paper towels. Grill (or broil on a broiler pan) on each side for 6 minutes for rare or 7 to 9 minutes for medium-rare. Transfer to a carving board and let stand for 8 to 10 minutes. Slice the meat at a 45-degree angle across the grain and serve with the horseradish sauce.

TO MAKE THE CREAMY HORSERADISH SAUCE: Whisk all the ingredients together until smooth and creamy. Put in the refrigerator for at least 4 hours to allow the flavors to meld. Serve in a ramekin beside the meat.

SERVES 6

Beef, Veal, and Chicken Meat Loaf

This hearty, homestyle meat loaf is a big success in our family. Whenever I make it, it disappears before my eyes!

2 stale kaiser rolls, broken into pieces

3 eggs, lightly beaten

1 pound ground beef

1 pound ground veal

1 pound ground chicken

1 medium onion, chopped

1¾ teaspoons Lawry's garlic salt

2 cups your favorite brand of canned tomato sauce

1 shredded carrot

1 shredded zucchini

4 ounces mushrooms, sliced (optional)

¾ cup bread crumbs

Salt and freshly ground black pepper

Preheat the oven to 350°F.

Soak the kaiser rolls in the eggs.

Combine the egg and bread mixture with the beef, veal, chicken, onion, 1 teaspoon of the garlic salt, tomato sauce (reserve some sauce to spread on top), carrot, zucchini, and, if desired, mushrooms.

Knead the mixture, shape it into a loaf, and place it on a baking sheet. Coat with the bread crumbs and the remaining ¾ teaspoon of garlic salt. Pour the remaining tomato sauce over the loaf.

Bake for 60 minutes and season with salt and pepper to taste.

SERVES 6

Baked White and Sweet Potato Wedges

Nonstick cooking spray

3 tablespoons olive oil

Salt and freshly ground black pepper

⅓ teaspoon paprika

3 large sweet potatoes, cut into ½-inch wedges

3 large baking potatoes, cut into ½-inch wedges

Preheat the oven to 475°F.

Lightly coat two baking sheets with cooking spray.

Mix the oil, salt, pepper, and paprika together. Toss the potatoes in seasoned oil until well coated. Arrange the wedges in a single layer on the baking sheets and bake until golden, 25 to 35 minutes, turning occasionally. Serve immediately.

SERVES 6

Herb-Roasted Organic Chicken

Aside from chicken soup's reputation as a remedy for the common cold, a roast chicken dinner probably comes closest to being considered a universal comfort meal. The sweet potato fritters give the meal an exciting twist. We have always loved this meal and continue to enjoy it to this day.

1 (3- to 4-pound) whole organic chicken

¼ cup olive oil

4 cloves garlic, peeled

2 lemons, cut into wedges

4 sprigs fresh rosemary

4 sprigs fresh thyme

4 fresh sage leaves

Paprika

Salt and freshly ground black pepper

About 1 cup chicken stock or water

Preheat the oven to 475°F.

Wash the chicken thoroughly and pat it dry, inside and out. Rub the oil over the inside and outside of the chicken. Stuff the garlic, lemons, and herbs inside the cavity. Rub the paprika, salt, and pepper over the outside of the chicken. Place the chicken, breast-side down, on a rack in a roasting pan. Cook in the center of the oven for about 25 minutes.

Carefully turn the chicken over and cook for 25 minutes more. At this point check to see if the chicken is cooked through by cutting between the thigh and the body; if the juices run clear it's done. If it is not completely cooked, lower the oven temperature to 350°F and cook for about 10 minutes more. Remove the chicken from the oven. Let it rest for 10 to 15 minutes before carving. Remove the garlic, lemon, and herbs, which can be used as garnish.

Deglaze the roasting pan with a little stock or water, stirring to scrape up the browned bits in the pan. This can be served in a small jug or gravy boat to accompany the chicken. Also serve with Fresh Applesauce (see page 228).

SERVES 6

Sweet Potato Fritters

3 sweet potatoes, peeled and grated

1 white potato, peeled and grated

1 medium onion, grated

2 tablespoons all-purpose flour

1 large egg, beaten

Pinch of salt and freshly ground black pepper

Safflower oil for shallow frying

Sour cream and crystallized ginger

In a large bowl, combine the sweet potatoes, white potato, onion, flour, egg, salt, and pepper, and stir together well.

Heat ¼ inch of oil in a large sauté pan. Drop ¼-cup measures of the batter into the pan. Do not overcrowd the pan. Fry until golden, about 2 to 3 minutes per side. Serve hot with sour cream and crystallized ginger.

SERVES 6 TO 8

Sunset Organic Chicken Pot Pie

4 tablespoons vegetable oil

3 tablespoons unsalted butter

1 onion, chopped

2 cloves garlic, chopped

2 leeks, whites only, sliced

3 cups sliced mushrooms

2 sprigs fresh thyme

¼ cup all-purpose flour

1 cup chicken stock

Salt and freshly ground black pepper

1 (3-pound) chicken, roasted, skinned, boned, and cubed

1 cup peas, blanched

1 carrot, diced and blanched

½ cup chopped fresh parsley

½ cup chopped fresh chives

3 sweet potatoes, baked

Preheat the oven to 350°F.

Add the oil and 2 tablespoons of the butter to a large sauté pan over medium heat. Sauté the onion, garlic, leeks, mushrooms, and thyme until tender. Add the flour and stir to make a roux. Cook for 2 minutes. Add the stock and stir until smooth; bring to a boil. Cook for about 10 minutes and season to taste with salt and pepper. Add the chicken, peas, carrot, parsley, and chives, and mix together to incorporate. Spoon into eight individual ramekins.

Remove and discard the skins from the sweet potatoes. Put the sweet potato flesh in a food processor with salt and pepper to taste and the remaining 1 tablespoon of butter and process until smooth. Smooth the sweet potato mixture decoratively on top of the chicken mixture in the ramekins and bake for 15 minutes. Place under the broiler until the tops are crisp.

SERVES 8

Beer-Batter Fish and Chips
with Homemade Tartar Sauce

FOR THE FISH

3 cups all-purpose flour

3 tablespoons olive oil

1 cup beer

1 egg white

Salt and freshly ground black pepper

Safflower oil

6 (6-ounce) cod fillets

Lemon wedges

FOR THE TARTAR SAUCE

1 cup mayonnaise

3 to 4 gherkins or cornichons,
finely chopped

1 teaspoon sweet pickle relish

1 tablespoon minced shallot

2 tablespoons fresh lemon juice
(optional)

Salt and freshly ground black pepper

TO MAKE THE FISH: Sift 1 cup of the flour into a bowl. Make a well in the center and pour in the olive oil; stir slowly to combine. Add a little beer at a time to make a batter consistency. Beat the egg white until stiff peaks form. Fold into the batter mixture. Add salt and pepper to taste.

Heat the safflower oil in a deep skillet to 375°F. Season the remaining 2 cups of flour with salt and pepper. Dredge the fish in the flour, then dip it in the batter and gently place it in the hot oil. Fry the fish until golden brown. Drain on paper towels. Serve with tartar sauce and lemon wedges.

TO MAKE THE TARTAR SAUCE: Mix all the ingredients together in a bowl. Check the seasoning and adjust as necessary. Refrigerate for at least 1 hour before serving.

SERVES 6

Crisp Matchstick Potatoes

3 large potatoes, washed and peeled

Vegetable oil

Salt

Cut the potatoes into ⅛-inch-thick matchstick slices using a mandoline. Keep them in a bowl of cold water. When ready to cook, drain the potatoes and dry them thoroughly on paper towels.

Heat the oil in a deep pot to 350° to 375°F. Fry the potatoes in batches until golden brown, 4 to 6 minutes. Using a slotted spoon, remove the potatoes from the pan and drain on paper towels.

Transfer the fries to a baking sheet and sprinkle them with salt while still hot. Keep warm in the oven at 250°F. When all the potatoes have been cooked, serve immediately.

SERVES 4

Shrimp and Scallop Burgers

Grilled Swordfish Steaks

6 (8-ounce) swordfish steaks

1½ tablespoons olive oil

1½ teaspoons paprika

Salt and freshly ground black pepper

Heat a grill to high.

Brush the fish with the oil and season with the paprika, salt, and pepper. Grill until flaky, 3 to 4 minutes on each side. Let stand for 5 minutes before serving.

SERVES 6

Shrimp and Scallop Burgers

Serve these with a side of Crisp Matchstick Potatoes (see page 110).

12 medium shrimp, peeled and deveined

12 sea scallops

2 cloves garlic, chopped

1 tablespoon chopped fresh ginger

1 cup chopped scallions

1 tablespoon sesame oil

2 tablespoons mirin

3 tablespoons soy sauce

Vegetable oil

Preheat the oven to 350°F.

Coarsely chop the shrimp and scallops in a food processor—do not overprocess. Transfer the seafood to a bowl and mix with the garlic, ginger, scallions, sesame oil, mirin, and soy sauce. Mold into four 1½-inch-thick burgers.

Heat a little vegetable oil in a sauté pan over medium heat and cook the burgers on both sides until golden, about 2 to 3 minutes per side. Transfer to a baking sheet and cook in the oven for 10 minutes, until cooked through. Serve with Avocado and Mango Dressing (see below).

SERVES 4

Avocado and Mango Dressing

2 avocados, pitted and peeled

2 tablespoons fresh lime juice

½ cup chopped scallions

1 mango, peeled, pitted, and chopped

3 tablespoons mirin

Salt and freshly ground black pepper

Puree the avocados in a food processor. Transfer to a small bowl and mix with the remaining ingredients.

Spaghetti with Clam Sauce

3 pounds littleneck clams

1 pound uncooked spaghetti

8 tablespoons extra-virgin olive oil

2 cloves garlic, thinly sliced

1 cup fresh bread crumbs

Salt and freshly ground black pepper

Pinch of crushed red pepper

½ cup clam juice

1 cup dry white wine

¼ cup chopped parsley

Soak the clams in cold water for 1 hour. Drain, then scrub well, discarding any clams that do not open when tapped.

Bring a large pot of salted water to a boil over high heat. Cook the spaghetti according to the package instructions until al dente.

Heat 3 tablespoons of the olive oil and half of the garlic in a large skillet over medium heat. Add the bread crumbs and cook, stirring frequently, until golden brown. Add salt and black pepper to taste and transfer to a bowl.

Heat the remaining 5 tablespoons olive oil, the remaining garlic, and the red pepper over medium heat. Cook until the garlic is golden brown.

Add the clams, clam juice, and wine, then cover and cook, shaking the pan often, until the clams have opened, about 5 minutes.

Remove the lid, increase the heat to high, and boil for 2 minutes. Stir in the parsley and add salt and black pepper to taste. Drain the spaghetti, then add it to the clams and toss to combine. Transfer to individual bowls and sprinkle each with toasted bread crumbs. Serve hot.

SERVES 4 TO 6

Hamptons Stuffed Eggplant

This can be made with or without bread crumbs, depending on the balance of the rest of the meal.

3 large eggplants, washed and dried

2½ teaspoons olive oil

2 cloves garlic, minced

½ cup finely chopped shallots

1 green bell pepper, diced

1 pound Roma tomatoes, coarsely chopped

¾ cup bread crumbs made from stale hard-crusted artisanal bread

½ cup freshly grated Parmesan cheese

⅓ cup finely chopped fresh basil

Salt and freshly ground black pepper

Preheat the oven to 350°F.

Prick the eggplants all over with a fork. Place them on a sheet pan and bake until almost cooked through, about 30 minutes Set aside to cool. When cool enough to handle, cut them in half lengthwise and scoop out the flesh, leaving ¼-inch-thick shells.

Heat the oil in a sauté pan over medium heat. Add the garlic, shallots, and bell pepper, and cook, stirring, until the shallots are translucent, about 5 minutes. Add the tomatoes and cook for 5 minutes. Add the flesh from the eggplant and cook for 3 to 5 minutes. Stir in the bread crumbs, ¼ cup of the cheese, and the basil. Season with salt and pepper to taste.

Spoon the mixture into the eggplant shells and arrange them in a glass baking dish, allowing the stuffing mixture to fall over the sides. Pour about ¼ inch of boiling water into the dish.

Sprinkle the remaining ¼ cup cheese on top. Bake until warmed through, about 20 minutes. If the pan starts to dry out during cooking, add a little more boiling water. Serve hot.

SERVES 6

Baby Shell Pasta with Fresh Tomato Sauce

2 pounds fresh plum tomatoes

16 ounces uncooked small shell pasta

6 tablespoons olive oil

3 cloves garlic, chopped

Pinch of crushed red pepper

½ medium onion, finely chopped

Salt

3 tablespoons chopped fresh basil

Peel the tomatoes by scoring the skin of each with a sharp knife. Place the tomatoes in a pot of boiling water and boil for approximately 1½ minutes, then remove them with a slotted spoon and plunge them into cold water. The skins will easily slip off. Chop and set aside.

In the meantime, cook the pasta al dente in boiling salted water for 8 to 10 minutes; drain.

Heat the oil in a saucepan over medium heat, then add the garlic and red pepper. Sauté until the garlic turns slightly golden. Add the chopped onion and sauté for another 2 minutes. Add the tomatoes and cook for 5 minutes. Add salt to taste. Add the chopped basil and a little more olive oil, then toss with the pasta. Serve.

SERVES 6

Phyllo Vegetable Stack

Try this with one of my favorite salads for a wonderful vegetarian meal: romaine, feta, cucumber, red and yellow peppers, black olives, tomatoes, watermelon, and pine nuts in a raspberry vinaigrette.

1 onion, finely chopped

2 cloves garlic, chopped

1 yellow zucchini, finely chopped

1 green zucchini, finely chopped

2 cups finely chopped eggplant

2 cups crimini mushrooms, finely chopped

4 tomatoes, chopped

4 tablespoons chopped fresh basil

2 sticks butter, melted

5 sheets phyllo pastry dough

Grated Parmesan cheese

Paprika

Preheat the oven to 400°F.

Sauté the onion in butter, then add the garlic. Add the zucchini, eggplant, and mushrooms, then the tomatoes and basil. Cook until the vegetables are soft. Add 1 tablespoon of Parmesan cheese. Set the vegetable mixture aside.

Brush butter on each sheet of phyllo pastry. Layer like a Napoleon, starting with the phyllo, then spooning the vegetable mixture on top and spreading it over the pastry dough. Then repeat. Finish with a layer of phyllo. Sprinkle the top layer with Parmesan and a dash of paprika. Cut the phyllo into 2-by-2-inch squares. Bake in a 400°F oven until golden brown, 12 to 15 minutes. Remove and serve warm. Stack three squares on top of one another to form a tower.

SERVES 4 TO 6

Desserts

Blueberry Crisp

Aunt Susan and I went blueberry-picking together with our young children in Amagansett. We decided to have a contest to see which team could pick the most berries. The smushed ones did not count. We had so much fun that we all forgot who won! I still remember how much we laughed. This crisp always reminds me of that magical day.

FOR THE BASE

3 cups fresh blueberries

2 tablespoons sugar

Juice and zest of 1 lemon

FOR THE CRISP TOPPING

¾ cup all-purpose flour

1 cup packed light brown sugar

1½ cups rolled oats

6 tablespoons (¾ stick) salted butter, softened

Preheat the oven to 375°F.

TO MAKE THE BASE: Toss the blueberries, sugar, lemon zest, and juice together in a bowl. Pour into a 9-inch square baking dish.

TO MAKE THE CRISP TOPPING: In a food-processor bowl, mix the flour, brown sugar, rolled oats, and butter and pulse until the mixture resembles crumbs. Spread this over the berries.

Bake until golden on top, 40 to 45 minutes.

SERVES 6

Cookies

I love chocolate! Deep, dark, rich chocolate! And with nuts! Oh, yes, even better. So does my family. When the boys were little, they would play baseball with their friends in the backyard. I would bring each of them a snack of chocolate milk and cookies to fortify their energy during breaks. Excited to resume the game, they would gulp it all down quickly and lick away the frothy moustaches that remained.

To create an even more indulgent treat, use these cookies to create ice cream sandwiches!

Chocolate Oatmeal Cookies

1 cup (2 sticks) salted butter

1 cup packed light brown sugar

½ cup granulated sugar

2 eggs

1 teaspoon vanilla extract

1¼ cups all-purpose flour

1 teaspoon baking soda

½ cup unsweetened cocoa

½ teaspoon salt

2 cups rolled oats

2 cups (12 ounces) dark chocolate chips

Preheat the oven to 350°F.

Cream the butter and both sugars together. Add the eggs and vanilla and beat until incorporated.

Sift the flour, baking soda, cocoa, and salt. Gradually add the dry ingredients to the butter mixture.

Add the oats and chocolate chips. Roll tablespoon-size balls and put them on a greased or parchment-lined cookie sheet.

Bake for 12 to 15 minutes.

MAKES 2 DOZEN

Chocolate Chocolate Nut Cookies

1 pound semisweet chocolate, chopped

4 tablespoons (½ stick) salted butter

¾ cup packed brown sugar

2 eggs

1 teaspoon pure vanilla extract

½ cup all-purpose flour

¼ teaspoon baking powder

¼ teaspoon salt

2 cups toasted walnuts or almonds, chopped

Preheat the oven to 350°F.

Melt half of the chopped chocolate with the butter in the top of a double boiler over simmering water. Let cool.

Mix in the sugar, eggs, and vanilla. In a small bowl, sift the flour, baking powder, and salt. Stir the dry ingredients into the melted chocolate mixture. Stir in the remaining chopped chocolate and the nuts. Cover the mixture and refrigerate for 1 hour.

Lightly butter two large baking sheets. Drop the batter in 2-tablespoon measures per cookie. Press down gently on each cookie. Bake until they're just starting to crack, 12 to 13 minutes.

Cool the cookies completely on the sheet. Remove and store in a cookie jar, or place in the freezer and serve cold.

MAKES 2 DOZEN

Chocolate Chocolate Nut Cookie Ice Cream Sandwiches

(First row, left to right): *Cemetery Gates* by Marc Chagall, ca. 1917. *Chocolate Grinder No.2* by Marcel Duchamp, ca. 1914. A portrait of French writer André Breton, ca. 1966. Roberto Matta, ca. 1957. (Second row, left to right): *The King and Queen Surrounded by Swift Nudes* by Marcel Duchamp, ca. 1912. *The Ship* by Salvador Dalí, ca. 1943. *Echo of Emptiness* by Salvador Dalí. (Third row, left to right): *Composition I* by Piet Mondrian being viewed in the private collection of Yves Saint Laurent and Pierre Berge. *Orthognonale* by Jean Hélion, ca. 1931. (Fourth row, left to right): Portrait of American abstract expressionist Robert Motherwell, February 18, 1962. *I and the Village* by Marc Chagall, ca. 1911. *Shop girls in the Garden of Tuileries* in 1929. (Fifth row, left to right): *Chess Players* by Marcel Duchamp, ca. 1911. "The Dunes" estate in East Hampton, ca. 1912. *Seated Woman in a Garden* by Pablo Picasso, ca. 1938.

The Artists

From December 1941 until the end of World War II, German U-boats attacked ships and tankers in American waters all along the eastern seaboard. As a result, the Coast Guard patrolled the shoreline of eastern Long Island, watching for enemy submarines.

As the situation in Europe began to deteriorate due to the Nazi occupation, many persecuted artists, architects, authors, and intellectuals fled their homelands and sought refuge in New York City. For some, the Hamptons offered a lifestyle they had enjoyed in their countries of origin, a respite from city life, a chance to commune with nature and each other, and an opportunity to have their creativity energized.

Painters such as surrealists[5] Marcel Duchamp, Fernand Léger, and Jean Hélion of France and Max Ernst of Germany were among those who arrived during this period. Modernist architects Antonin Raymond of Czechoslovakia, Pierre Chareau of France, Peter Blake of Germany, and Paul Lester Wiener and Bernard Rudofsky of Austria also arrived on our welcoming shores. The American editor Varian Fry[6] aided and housed many of the émigrés in Marseilles before helping them escape from the Nazis to New York, among them artists Marc Chagall and Ernst, writer Hannah Arendt, and sculptor Jacques Lipchitz. They came to New York and then to the Hamptons, where their work continued to evolve.

Gerald and Sara Murphy were among the American expatriates who resided in Paris in the 1920s, living a Bohemian lifestyle and befriending many of the pioneer artists and authors of the Modern Movement. Sara was the daughter of Frank B. Wiborg, a self-made millionaire who made his fortune in ink manufacturing and printmaking. He built a family estate called "The Dunes," a sprawling oceanfront home in East Hampton. The couples' progressive attitude toward the arts and literature attracted the newly arrived European émigrés, and they welcomed them to stay in their spacious home. Their huge estate became a haven for artists and authors. Their friends included Ernest Hemingway, Gertrude Stein, F. Scott Fitzgerald, Pablo Picasso, Chagall, André Masson, Léger, and his companion, the Lebanese artist Lucia Christofanetti.

Léger and Christofanetti, enchanted by the area, ultimately rented in neighboring Amagansett. Max Ernst and his partner, Dorothea Tanning, the American artist and writer, shared the rented property with them. Their guests were artists from all over the globe: surrealists Salvador Dalí of Spain, Yves Tanguy of France, and Roberto Matta of Cuba; abstract expressionist[7] Arshile Gorky of Armenia; Japanese-American sculptor Isamu Noguchi; Dutch neo-plasticist[8] painter Piet Mondrian; and Cuban-French writer Anaïs Nin.

---

[5]Surrealism: a movement in visual art and literature developed principally in twentieth-century Europe, between World Wars I and II, out of the Dada movement. It stressed elements of surprise, unexpected juxtapositions, and defied reason, relying heavily on imagery and exploration of the effects of chance. Surrealists regarded their work as an expression of the philosophical movement. The poet and critic André Breton was a major spokesman of the movement and published "The Surrealist Manifesto" in 1924.
[6]Varian Fry: A Taft School and Harvard University–educated American journalist who ran a rescue network in Vichy, France, that helped thousands of anti-Nazi and Jewish refugees to escape from the Nazis. Not until 1991 were his courageous actions acknowledged when he received his first official recognition from a United States agency, the United States Holocaust Memorial Council. However, the "American Schindler" died in obscurity in 1967. Source: www.almondseed.com/vfry/.

French surrealist writer-poet André Breton (the "father" of the movement) also came to the Hamptons. The newly arrived émigrés socialized with the American abstract-expressionist sculptor David Hare and painter/printmaker Robert Motherwell. This international group included the surrealist painters Enrico Donati from Italy and Sonia Sekula from Switzerland, Romanian architect Frederick Kiesler, and Cuban artist Wifredo Lam. The Hamptons had become the mecca for artistic, literary, and architectural modernism[9]: a breeding ground for the free-flowing exchange of ideas.

There had been a quiet period in the art world of the Hamptons from the early 1920s until the coming of this new generation of artists after World War II. Their arrival carried a substantial impact that would redefine the Hamptons. It was during this time that the New York School of abstractionism was instrumental in refocusing the attention of the art world away from Paris and toward New York.

After the war some of the European surrealists made their way back to Europe. In America, abstract expressionism was becoming the new form of artistic expression. Many artists came out to the Hamptons either to visit or to make it their permanent home.

Painter Jackson Pollock, a major force in the American abstract-expressionist movement, came to the Hamptons with his wife, the artist Lee Krasner, in 1946. Painter and printmaker Mark Rothko also came in 1946. The painter John Little came in 1947, and

artists Willem and Elaine de Kooning and Italian sculptor Constantino Nivola came out in 1948. Balcomb Greene and his wife, Gertrude Glass, who was also an artist, purchased land at Montauk Point in 1947. Alfonso Ossorio arrived in East Hampton in 1949. Franz Kline found the Hamptons in 1950. Artists Theodoros Stamos, Conrad Marca-Relli, and Cubist[10] sculptor Jacques Lipchitz came in 1954.

Other American artists who frequented the Hamptons during this period were William Baziotes, Helen Frankenthaler, Adolph Gottlieb, Jimmy Ernst, John Ferren, and sculptor–modernist painter Wilfred Zogbaum. Joining them were sculptor Ibram Lassaw, landscape painter–watercolorist Nell Blaine, and contemporary realist painter Jane Freilicher. In addition, gallery owners and art dealers Leo Castelli and David Porter also were drawn to the Hamptons.

American muralist–abstract painter James Brooks chose the cliffs of Montauk. Sag Harbor became the home for genre portraitist Alexander Brook in 1948, as well as modernist Gina Knee and Val Telberg, the Russian surrealist photomontagist–avant-garde filmmaker, in 1956.

For the most part, in the early days the artists could not afford beachfront homes, so they found private havens where the prices were very low. They had talent but no money, and they were on their way to achieving recognition.

Motherwell, a discovery of Peggy Guggenheim's, was one of the first abstract-

---

[7]Abstract expressionism: An American postwar art movement that was influential worldwide. With New York replacing Paris as the center of the art world, this style dominated art until the dawn of Pop Art in the 1960s. The artists expressed spontaneity and freedom of spirit, often painting on huge canvases, using large brushes and allowing drips to contribute to the work in an effort to show their emotions.

[8]Neo-plasticism: Founded by Dutch painter Theo van Doesburg on the belief that for artists the only absolutes of life were vertical and horizontal lines painted in primary colors and shades of black, gray, and white. Van Doesburg and Piet Mondrian were the two main painters of this movement.

[9]Modernism: The movement in architecture, design, and art between the two wars (1918–1939). Its proponents sought creative means to express the world in response to the violence and destruction that had resulted from World War I.

[10]Cubism: An art movement started by Pablo Picasso and Georges Braque between 1907 and 1914. Picasso's *Les Demoiselles d'Avignon* is often cited as the the first piece of Cubist art. Objects were interpreted into geometric shapes and cubes and often fractured. Later Cubist painters include Fernand Léger, Marcel Duchamp, Juan Gris, and Diego Rivera.

expressionist artists to summer in the Hamptons. He came to visit Max Ernst, the Dadaist and surrealist artist who had settled in Amagansett a few years earlier. Motherwell commissioned a house and studio of his own in 1945 to be built in East Hampton.

Pollock and Krasner purchased a simple, unheated farmhouse in the rustic hamlet of Springs after visiting Motherwell. Pollock painted allover abstractions inspired by nature. Krasner's work often reflected the seasons and the cycles of life, using plant life as her metaphor.

Elaine and Willem de Kooning visited the Pollocks in 1948 and fell in love with the area. They in turn rented the Red House in Bridgehampton, introducing contemporaries and fellow abstract-expressionist painters Ludwig Sander, Perle Fine, and Nicolas Carone to it. The de Koonings moved to East Hampton permanently in 1963 and purchased a house there in 1976.

Another contemporary of theirs, Nivola, moved from New York to the Hamptons permanently in 1948 with his wife, Ruth, and their children. They restored an eighteenth-century farmhouse and barn in East Hampton by removing its interior partitions. They painted the remaining walls white and the floors a bright New York–taxicab yellow. Nivola's landscape design incorporated his talents as a painter, sculptor, and architect to create a garden of open-air spaces with free-standing walls, fences, and natural plantings connected by paths to function as defined rooms for gatherings with friends and family. He collaborated with his friend Austrian architect Bernard Rudofsky, on the floor plans for the garden. This modernistic expression of an "outdoor house" merged architecture and landscape design, and included many of Nivola's own sculptures, which he distributed around the property.

Admiring guests included Pollock, Krasner, de Kooning, Rothko, Kline, and Brooks, and photographer Hans Namuth, along with Dorothy Norman, who was also a photographer, author, editor, and patron of the arts, as well as illustrator-cartoonist Saul Steinberg and his wife, the abstract expressionist Hedda Sterne.[11] Architects Peter Blake, Frederick Kiesler, and Paul Lester Weiner and real-estate developer Paul Tishman were also guests. In 1950 another guest, Charles Édouard Jeanneret—the famous Le Corbusier—visited them, admired their home, and suggested that a mural might be a nice addition. Nivola offered two plaster walls in the old farmhouse, upon which Le Corbusier painted a two-part mural that took him one week to complete. Nivola's garden continued to expand and became his experimental laboratory. In the 1950s Nivola discovered a system of sandcasting while playing with his children on the beach. He poured liquid plaster into negative forms that he had dug into the wet sand. When these had set, he removed the resulting castings and painted them with water-based colors. He patented the method and refined the technique in his studio on the property.

Alfonso Ossorio, a wealthy patron of the arts and a friend of Pollock and Krasner, came to the Hamptons from the Philippines in 1949. In 1952 he purchased "The Creeks" and generously invited such avant-garde artists as Clyfford Still, Grace Hartigan, Syd Solomon, Joseph Glasco, and sculptor George Spaventa to work in his studios and develop their ideas.

[11]Hedda Sterne: The only female member of The Irascibles.
[12]Abstractionism: art that does not represent recognizable objects.

Abstractionism[12] came to the Guild Hall, which was by now established as the great cultural center of the area, in the form of an exhibition in 1949 entitled *17 Artists of Eastern Long Island.* Organized by Lucia Christofanetti of Amagansett and Roseanne Larkin of East Hampton, it featured the work of Jackson Pollock, Raphael Soyer, and Ray Prohaska. The Guild Hall also hosted *10 East Hampton Abstractionists* in 1950, an exhibition featuring Pollock, Krasner, Motherwell, and James Brooks, among others. Another exhibition called *The Sea Around Us* in 1953 featured Pollock, Stamos, and Baziotes. Newspapers and magazines covered the exhibitions and elaborated on the excitement that these artists had brought to the area, resulting in an influx of new arrivals. Tourism thrived. Everyone wanted to see where and how the avant-garde lived.

Fairfield Porter, a painter of idyllic land-scapes and portraits, and his wife, Anne, a poet, attracted a number of controversial and sometimes unconventional house guests to join the community of artists and authors in Southampton. The artists Larry Rivers and Jane Freilicher, realist painter John Button, landscape painter turned abstractionist Robert Dash, and the writer and composer John Gruen and his wife, the artist Jane Wilson, were among them. The relation-ships among the avant-garde set served as a conduit to cross-pollinate ideas between the artistic and literary worlds. Creative people came from all parts of the Hamptons to social gatherings and parties at artists' studios and to enjoy annual picnics on the Coast Guard Beach in East Hampton.

The work of abstract expressionists Pollock, Krasner, and de Kooning demonstrate

a subjectivity regarding the expression of their relationship to the environment. In contrast to this, Pop artists in the 1960s and '70s, such as Jim Dine, James Rosenquist, Roy Lichtenstein, and Andy Warhol, were unattached and cool in their expression. Nevertheless these artists, too, came to the Hamptons to find a remote refuge.

Dine lived in East Hampton from 1962 to 1968. He would visit the local supply stores that provided tools for the needs of fishermen, farmers, carpenters, and maintenance workers of East Hampton, and use the implements he purchased to develop much of his artwork.

Rosenquist moved to East Hampton in 1967. His specialty was to combine or overlap familiar everyday images that he had distorted and fragmented, and adhere them onto a canvas to create an interesting narrative. "Seemingly unrelated images [were juxtaposed] in order to make a poignant statement." Lichtenstein and his wife, Dorothy, found the comfort of home in a 1910 carriage house in Southampton on posh Gin Lane in 1971. His Benday dots[13] and comic-book-style letter-ing and speech balloons were inspired by one of his sons, who challenged him one day to improve upon a Mickey Mouse comic strip.

In 1972 Warhol, with his partner, the movie director Paul Morrissey, bought a twenty-acre ocean-front estate in Montauk, one of the Seven Sisters that had been built by Stanford White in 1880, and named it Eothen (Greek for "from the East"). However, most of the time it was rented out to tenants such as Lee Radziwill, Mick and Bianca Jagger, Halston, Elizabeth Taylor, Peter Brant and Stephanie Seymour, Julian Schnabel, and Bruce Weber. It is unlikely that Warhol ever produced any artwork there. Julian Schnabel rented the

[13]Benday dots: a printing process that combines two or more different-colored small dots to create a third color.

Warhol estate in 1983, until he purchased another Stanford White–designed house in 1998. He built an outdoor studio in 2001.

In 1972 Peter Beard became one of the first famous photographers to settle in the Hamptons. As well as for his nature and fashion photography, he is known as an artist, diarist, world traveler, and champion of wildlife conservation. Beard has owned his house on Montauk Point for more than forty-five years.

The renowned photo-realist[14] painter, photographer, and printmaker Chuck Close has owned a home in Bridgehampton since the mid-1970s, though he still maintains a studio in New York City.

David Salle, another influential and controversial star of the neo-expressionist movement, lived and worked in Sagaponack from 1990 to 2004. In 2005 he bought a home in East Hampton, where he continues to produce his art.

Ross Bleckner is a Long Island native whose work combines abstract expression-ism, minimalism, and op art. In 1992 he bought Truman Capote's modern saltbox house in Sagaponack. Since then he has renovated and enlarged the house and added an adjoining studio, where he continues to live and work.

It is said that the Hamptons have a unique quality of light, which is perhaps why the area has inspired April Gornick, who was influenced by the Luminist school.[15] She is one of the most celebrated landscape painters of her generation. Her husband

is the artist Eric Fischl, best known as a figurative painter who often depicts people in natural settings. Since 1986 Gornik and Fischl have made their residence in the Hamptons, first in Sag Harbor, then in North Haven.

In recent years other artists have been drawn to the Hamptons. Abstract sculptor John Chamberlain, painters Donald Baechler and Richmond Burton, and photographer Ralph Gibson are among them. John Chamberlain first visited the Hamptons in 1957 and stayed with his friend, the artist Larry Rivers. It wasn't until 1992 that he moved to the Hamptons, stayed in a house in Northwest Woods, and worked in a studio once owned by Elaine de Kooning. Chamberlain sold this in the 1990s to fellow artist Richmond Burton. And so these historical properties of significance and artistic provenance are often found in the ownership of those who hope to inherit inspiration from what has passed before, as if there were magical spirits or muses residing within the walls.

New artists continue the pilgrimage to the East End, keeping the community thriving with new talent. Some of these notables are Eric Freeman, George Condo, Cindy Sherman, Ned Smyth, and Rima Mardoyan-Smyth, to name but a few. Almost all of the artists from the 1970s until now still produce art in the Hamptons, making it one of the most creative and prolific artists' colonies to date.

[14]Photo-realism: art movement in the late '60s to early '70s in which paintings resemble and give the illusion of a photograph. The forerunners and best-known artists of this movement include Chuck Close and Richard Estes.
[15]Luminism: an American landscape painting style popular from the 1850s to the 1870s characterized by the effects of the light in landscape through using aerial perspective and emphasizing tranquility, and often depicting calm water and a soft, hazy day.

CHAPTER 3

East Hampton

When our daughter, Dylan, was born, we found a lovely shingled saltbox house with symmetrical additions on either side of the original structure, directly on the ocean (i.e., on the second dune in East Hampton). The house had leaded-glass windows and was furnished with authentic Early American furniture, portraits, artifacts, and other décor. It was a large house with plenty of room for the baby to have a tiny bedroom for her crib, dressing table, and wardrobe; for the nanny to have her own bedroom and for the boys to share a room, which I always liked them to do. There was also a large bathroom with a wonderful skylight and a big claw-foot tub where the children could be bathed.

On the main floor there was a large eat-in kitchen with a long wooden table and chairs at the bay casement windows facing the ocean.

Ricky Lauren, East Hampton, 1975.

The walls were made of red brick, and the cabinets were dark pine. A large wooden prep table stood in the middle of this ample kitchen. On the brick wall opposite, there was a huge black potbellied stove with copper pots hanging from an iron pot rack extending outward from the wall. The vaulted wooden ceiling was of double height with beams running across it.

There were four doors in the kitchen. One led outside to the yard and a pebbled driveway, where we kept our white Jeep for tooling around on the beach and our convertible that took us back and forth to the city. Another door led to an outdoor brick dining terrace, and a third door led to a formal dining room, which I converted into a cheerful and lovely playroom for the children. I filled it with games, toys, building blocks, doll carriages, and bicycles. The last door in the kitchen led to the basement stairs.

We named the guest room adjacent to the playroom "Nana's room," since my mother and her dog were its occupants most of the time. At the first hint of daylight, my mother loved to walk her dog in the fresh morning seaside air. She would then brew fragrant Viennese coffee before starting to cook for later in the day. I can still smell the wonderful aroma of meatballs and fresh tomato sauce that greeted me along with the coffee. She was happy to delight us with one of the homey meals that I've loved since childhood.

The atmosphere in the living room needed to be lightened up. I achieved this by storing two huge Early American hook rugs, along with a number of austere portraits of Pilgrims and seafaring ancestors, safely in the attic. I removed the old chintz fabric from the couches and wing chair to expose the clean white muslin underpinning, and I draped some of my Indian blankets over them. I also recruited a wooden coffee table and two worn leather Barcelona chairs from another part of the room. Underneath all of this I placed a new sisal rug, to create a cozy seating area around the hearth.

Behind one of the couches was an ancient, out-of-tune black baby-grand piano, which served many functions.

It became the stand for our 16-millimeter film projector, from which we often showed movies for our family and guests. With a free-standing pull-down screen, our living room was converted into a screening room! We have so many memories of friends and family laughing and crying together, caught up in the emotions aroused by the classic films that we all watched and adored.

*David (age 3), Ralph,
Andrew (age 6), Ricky,
and Dylan (age 1½),
East Hampton, summer 1975.*

Dylan, Andrew, and David,
East Hampton, 1977.

The patio outside our living room had a low wall of flat stones around a rectangular terrace. The wall was an excellent place for perching. To turn the patio into a lounging area, we placed denim-covered mats against the inner walls and added tray tables. To this we added a multitude of bright-colored throw pillows. We often picnicked there under huge Italian Veronese marketplace umbrellas. If it rained, we could pile everything indoors to suggest sofas in an empty corner of the living room.

We spent eleven wonderful years in this house. At one point we put in a swimming pool, which we sited on the lawn just a few grassy steps from the lounge terrace, with a wonderful vista of the dunes and the ocean.

There was an expanse of lush green grass that bordered the rows of Rosa rugosa bushes that created a boundary between our landscaped area and the natural plants of the dunes. Nearly hidden between the Rosa rugosa bushes were some narrow rugged steps that were made out of railroad ties. At the bottom of the steps was a bunker-like shower entrenched in the hillside of our lawn. Ralph, the children, and I would shower there on our way back from the beach before reentering the house. From the bottom of the steps, a path with beach grasses on either side meandered over this dune, which led us to the wide Atlantic seacoast beach.

Our house stood on a property with six other houses. All were tucked back toward the ocean from the county road, with a large field in between that was tended by a local farmer who planted potatoes, corn, and cantaloupes. The private roads on the property along the side of the field were lined with pine, apple, and cherry trees. The blossoms in the springtime were pink and profuse, and the fruit at the end of the summer and in early fall was delicious. We regularly dined on the fresh corn and potatoes that we picked from the field ourselves just before we prepared our dinners.

Because of our distance from the main thoroughfare, the roads all around us were safe for the children to play upon and ride their bicycles. I recall the children's red plastic motorcycle that was bleached pink by the sun, the red-and-blue Noddy car, the red-and-yellow Big Wheel, the first two-wheelers, and, as time went by— the go-cart!

At the back of the house, facing away from the ocean, was a large lawn, which we used as a playing field for many a fever-pitched softball game. There was Frisbee, badminton, Wiffle baseball, and volleyball. Indoor entertainment consisted of block-building, painting, coloring, and playing with stuffed animals, cars, and trucks. There were plenty of fun things to do without TV until nighttime, when we all sat together and watched. These were the days of young family life and socializing with new friends, and the meals we enjoyed reflected that.

Fun with Pots and Pans

When the children were very small, I used to assemble various pots, pans, lids, cooking utensils, and wooden spoons for play. We tried them on as hats and used them as musical instruments. Then we would have a big parade of our own. We had great fun marching and singing and playing our instruments.

Andrew's Turtle

We bought Andrew a turtle when he was nine. It was quite a big one, about six inches long. He kept him in a large glass terrarium and fed him lettuce, bananas, and cooked chopped meat. Andrew's responsibility was to feed and exercise the turtle and to clean the turtle's home. Twice a week, he used four rolls of paper towels and a bottle of Windex, in order to do a meticulous job.

The turtle lived in the playroom in our city apartment for two years. In the summertime, he would travel and vacation with us in East Hampton. At the end of one summer, we asked Andrew if he could let his pet go free. With great ceremony and many tears, Andrew let him wander out over the lawn for the last time. He pronounced some sacred words just before "Alvin" disappeared into the tangle of wildly overgrown Rosa rugosa and shrubs that separated our house from the beach.

One sunny summer afternoon, nearly a year later, we spotted a turtle out on the lawn in exactly the same place where Andrew had fed Alvin so many times before. We rushed out with bananas and lettuce to celebrate the happy reunion. As he snubbed our offer and continued to make his way across the lawn, we watched him stop every now and then to sample the delicate clover leaves instead.

Off into the sunset he trudged, and we were never really sure that this indeed was our beloved Alvin. We never saw or heard from him again—not even a postcard!

Snow-Covered East Hampton

One year we had lots of snow. The potato field next to our house was buried under it. We had a new white Jeep, and our caretaker hitched a homemade sled to the back of it. We all donned our snowsuits and spent many happy hours coasting around that field on our lovely sled as we sang at the top of our lungs, "Oh, what fun it is to ride in a one-Jeep open sleigh!"

Lunch on the Go

To make an adventure out of the children's lunchtime, it was fun for them to pretend that they were heading off to some imaginary place with their lunches packed to go. Sometimes each of them carried their own favorite to the beach or to the grassy lawn under a tree. I would fill their various lunch pails, baskets, or superhero lunchboxes with all kinds of goodies and snacks, like peanut butter and jelly and sliced bananas on toasted cinnamon-raisin bread, or tuna fish and celery on seeded rye or bagels. For dessert I packed cookies with fresh summertime fruit, like cherries, peaches, nectarines, or plums. Chocolate or strawberry milk—"The Pink Bunny Drink"—filled each Thermos.

Fresh Catch

I remember witnessing what was for me an amazing summertime phenomenon on the beach in East Hampton: Schools of weakfish were jumping out of the ocean and landing on the shoreline, probably after being chased by bigger fish or roped in by fishermen's nets, or a combination of the two. The fish were still alive and flopping around on the sand. Andrew was about ten years old at the time. He grabbed one of the fish by the tail and carried it up to the house. His strong, determined little body struggled to carry it there because it was pretty heavy, weighing at least fifteen pounds. On the way up, it bit him on the calf, and he still bears the scar. Once we had it up at the house, it was subject to my recently learned skills of scaling, deboning, and preparing fillets, which I broiled for our dinner that night. The flavor was perfect. We truly enjoyed our "fresh catch" of the sea.

Assorted Pastry Basket

Breakfasts

Assorted Pastry Basket

Ricky's Favorite Corn Muffins

Sunrise Granola

Assorted Pastry Basket

Serve these pastries with granola, fresh-squeezed orange juice, and your favorite hot breakfast beverage.

Fruit Scones

2 cups all-purpose flour

⅓ cup sugar, plus more for sprinkling

1 teaspoon baking powder

1 teaspoon baking soda

½ teaspoon salt

½ cup (1 stick) unsalted butter (frozen)

½ cup fat-free plain yogurt

1 large egg

Fresh seasonal fruit (peaches or blueberries)

Preheat the oven to 400°F.

In a bowl, mix the flour, sugar, baking powder, baking soda, and salt. Using a coarse grater, shred the butter into the flour mixture. Use your fingers to mix the butter in. The mixture should resemble coarse meal.

In a separate bowl, whisk the yogurt and the egg together. Using a fork, mix the yogurt mixture into the flour mixture. Use your hands to fold in the fruit until it becomes a dough. It may seem dry, but there is enough liquid to turn it into a dough.

On a lightly floured surface, roll out the dough into a circle about ¾ inch thick. Sprinkle with some sugar and cut the dough into triangles. Place each triangle on a cookie sheet lined with parchment paper. Bake for about 23 to 25 minutes. Serve warm or at room temperature.

MAKES 6 TO 8 SCONES

Mixed Berry, Apple, and Oat Muffins

6 tablespoons (¾ stick) unsalted butter, melted

1 cup firmly packed light brown sugar

½ cup low-fat milk

1 large egg

1 cup all-purpose flour

1½ teaspoons baking powder

1 teaspoon ground cinnamon

½ teaspoon salt

½ cup rolled oats

½ cup grated apple

½ cup fresh blueberries

½ cup fresh raspberries

Preheat the oven to 400°F. Grease a standard-size 12-cup muffin pan.

Put the butter in a large bowl. Add the brown sugar, milk, and egg and mix well.

Sift the flour, baking powder, cinnamon, and salt together and add to the milk mixture; mix just until blended. Fold in the oats, apple, and berries. Pour the batter into the prepared muffin pan.

Bake until a toothpick inserted in a muffin comes out clean, 25 to 30 minutes. Turn out of the pan and let cool on a wire rack, then serve.

MAKES 12 MUFFINS

Coffee Cake with Crumb

1½ cups all-purpose flour

¼ cup packed light brown sugar

2 teaspoons baking powder

½ teaspoon baking soda

½ teaspoon salt

½ cup sour cream

⅓ cup buttermilk

2 tablespoons vegetable oil

1 egg yolk

1 teaspoon vanilla extract

2 large egg whites

FOR THE CRUMB MIX

¼ cup all-purpose flour

¼ cup packed light brown sugar

½ teaspoon ground cinnamon

3 tablespoons butter

Grease and flour a Bundt pan. Preheat the oven to 350°F. Sift the flour, sugar, baking powder, baking soda, and salt into a bowl.

In a separate bowl, mix the sour cream, buttermilk, oil, egg yolk, and vanilla and whisk thoroughly until completely blended.

Add the milk mixture to the flour mixture. Beat the egg whites until stiff peaks form. Gently fold the whites into the batter. Pour half of the batter into the prepared pan.

MAKE THE CRUMB MIX: Put the flour, brown sugar, and cinnamon in a small bowl. Cut in the butter until thoroughly mixed. Sprinkle the crumb mix on top of the batter. Pour the remaining batter on top of all of this. Bake until a toothpick inserted in the center comes out clean, 35 to 40 minutes.

SERVES 10

Ricky's Favorite Corn Muffins

When I recall my childhood I remember my mother busy in the kitchen preparing all the desserts and baked goods that we ate in our home. She was an amazing baker and we had lovely breakfast treats and desserts on a regular basis. Her baked goods were the only ones I knew. Then one day for some reason that I cannot recall, she brought home a package of store-bought corn muffins. Just like a typical child I marveled at the taste and the texture of the packaged corn muffins. I, who had a mother who made elaborate European pastries, was intrigued by the commercial muffin!

Years later when I had my own children my need for shortcuts for the busy mother drew me once again to consider the corn muffin. Simple, homey, and American, I thought as I tried all the resources and became obsessed to find the perfect recipe. I even asked everyone to try their hand. Finally, I am pleased to present my favorite recipe to you!

1½ cups all-purpose flour

1 cup sugar

¾ cup cornmeal

1 tablespoon baking powder

1 teaspoon salt

2 eggs

1 cup low-fat milk

½ cup (1 stick) salted butter, melted

Nonstick cooking spray

Preheat the oven to 400°F. Combine the dry ingredients in a bowl. Combine the eggs and milk and mix lightly. Pour the melted butter and milk mixture into the dry ingredients at the same time and mix until just blended.

Spray a 12-cup muffin pan with cooking spray and evenly distribute the batter among the cups (approximately 2 ounces of batter per cup). Bake until a toothpick inserted into a muffin comes out clean, 20 to 25 minutes. Serve with strawberry preserves, fresh butter, and ripe strawberries.

MAKES 12 MUFFINS

Sunrise Granola

6 cups rolled oats (not quick-cooking or instant)

2 cups mixed nuts and seeds: sunflower seeds, chopped walnuts, pecans, almonds, and cashews

1 teaspoon ground cinnamon

Pinch of salt

½ cup honey or maple syrup

1 cup raisins or chopped dried fruit

Preheat the oven to 350°F. In a large bowl, combine the oats, nuts and seeds, cinnamon, salt, and honey or maple syrup. Spread the mixture on a rimmed sheet pan and bake for 30 to 35 minutes, stirring occasionally. The mixture should brown evenly without burning.

Remove from the oven and add the dried fruit. Cool on a rack, stirring occasionally, until the granola is cooled to room temperature. Stored in a sealed container in the refrigerator, it will keep indefinitely. Serve with homemade or Greek yogurt and fresh fruit.

MAKES 8 CUPS

Luncheon

Cold Poached Salmon with Dill Sauce

Country Chicken Chili

Feta Cheese and Spinach Phyllo Purses

Watermelon and Arugula Salad

Dylan's Sunshine Salad with Mango Dressing

Cold Poached Salmon
with Dill Sauce

FOR THE SALMON

1 cup chicken stock

1 cup water

Juice of 1 lemon

3 sprigs fresh thyme

2 bay leaves

6 (6- to 8-ounce) salmon fillets

FOR THE DILL SAUCE

½ cup sour cream

½ tablespoon Dijon mustard

1 tablespoon fresh lemon juice

2 teaspoons chopped fresh dill

TO MAKE THE SALMON: In a large pan or Dutch oven, bring the stock, water, lemon juice, thyme, and bay leaves to a boil. Add the salmon, lower the heat to medium-low, and cover. Cook until the salmon is cooked through and a knife can be easily inserted in the center, 10 to 15 minutes.

Put the salmon in a large bowl and pour the poaching liquid over it. Refrigerate overnight.

TO MAKE THE DILL SAUCE: Whisk all the ingredients together until well blended. Chill for at least 1 hour.

Remove the salmon from the poaching liquid and serve with the sauce.

SERVES 6

Country Chicken Chili

Serve this warm, spicy chili with leftover corn muffins from breakfast (see page 142).

2 to 2½ pounds ground chicken

¼ cup vegetable oil

Salt and freshly ground black pepper

1 onion, chopped

3 cloves garlic, chopped

½ cup diced carrots

½ cup diced celery

1 red bell pepper, seeded and chopped

1 yellow bell pepper, seeded and chopped

½ chipotle chili in adobo, minced

2 tablespoons tomato paste

2 (28-ounce) cans crushed tomatoes

1 bay leaf

1 teaspoon ground cumin

1 teaspoon dried oregano

1 cup cooked chickpeas

1 cup chopped scallions

1 cup chopped fresh parsley

In a large saucepan over medium heat, sauté the chicken in a little oil for about 8 minutes and season to taste with salt and pepper. Remove from the pan and set aside.

Add a little more oil to the same pan, and sauté the onion, garlic, carrots, and celery until soft, about 5 minutes. Add the peppers, chipotle, tomato paste, crushed tomatoes, bay leaf, cumin, and oregano. Cook for 10 minutes. Add the chickpeas and chicken. Continue cooking for 15 minutes longer. Add the scallions and parsley and serve.

SERVES 6

Feta Cheese and Spinach Phyllo Purses

I serve these purses one per plate, surrounded by the colorful Watermelon and Arugula Salad. I include a slice of melon for more color.

1 pound fresh spinach

1 teaspoon salt

½ cup chopped onion

1 teaspoon unsalted butter

4 cloves garlic, chopped

2 ounces feta cheese, crumbled

36 (9-inch) square sheets phyllo dough, covered with damp cloth

Nonstick olive oil spray

Cook the spinach in salted water until just warm, not cooked. Drain and press out the water.

Sauté the onion in the butter over medium heat and add the garlic. Cook until the onion is translucent. Stir into the spinach and add the cheese.

Preheat the oven to 400°F. Spray one sheet of phyllo with olive oil. Layer with another square of phyllo, at a 45-degree angle to the first. Continue with two more pieces, spraying each piece. Press them into a 4-inch tart pan. Top with ¾ cup of the spinach filling. Bring the corners to the center and give a little twist to close the top. Repeat with the remaining phyllo and filling. Bake until golden brown, 15 to 18 minutes. Serve hot.

SERVES 9

Watermelon and Arugula Salad

1½ cups balsamic vinegar

1½ tablespoons honey

9 cups seeded watermelon, cut into 1-inch cubes

1½ cups crumbled feta cheese

9 cups baby arugula

¾ cup toasted pine nuts

In a saucepan, cook the vinegar until it is reduced to ¾ cup. Add the honey.

In a large bowl, combine the watermelon and cheese. Pile the arugula on serving plates and top with the watermelon-and-cheese mixture. Sprinkle with the pine nuts and drizzle with the vinegar mixture.

SERVES 9

Dylan's Sunshine Salad
with Mango Dressing

When Dylan was a little girl, she wanted to make a special lunch for her mommy and daddy and her two older brothers. She enlisted the help of her babysitter and presented us with her special "sunshine salad," so named because each food item was arranged on the platter to look like the rays of the sun. When Dylan first created it, most of the foods she chose to eat were "sunny" yellow or "happy" orange. This was before she discovered turquoise blue, which has since become her favorite color, though it is definitely not a common color for food. In our household, the sunshine salad has evolved over time. Color and nutritional value have been scrutinized and adjusted, but we have kept the sunshine theme going!

This salad is a good way to use up leftover roast chicken, which is easier to slice if it has been refrigerated overnight.

FOR THE SALAD

1 head green-leaf lettuce, leaves separated and washed

1 head red-leaf lettuce, leaves separated and washed

1 chicken breast, roasted and cooled

1 mango, peeled, pitted, and sliced

1 papaya, peeled, seeded and sliced

1 red bell pepper, seeded and sliced

1 yellow bell pepper, seeded and sliced

1 cup roasted macadamia nuts

½ cup sliced water chestnuts, drained

1 cup raisins

FOR THE DRESSING

1¾ pounds mangos, peeled, pitted, and chopped

¼ cup cider vinegar

1 tablespoon Dijon mustard

1 teaspoon curry powder

½ cup sunflower oil

½ teaspoon honey

TO MAKE THE SALAD: Arrange the lettuce leaves around a large serving platter. Remove the skin from the chicken and cut the meat off the bones; slice the chicken very thinly. Arrange the chicken, mango, papaya, peppers, nuts, water chestnuts, and raisins "like the rays of the sun" around the platter.

Drizzle with the dressing and serve.

TO MAKE THE DRESSING: Puree the mangos, vinegar, mustard, and curry powder together in a blender or food processor. Transfer to a bowl and whisk in the oil and honey.

SERVES 4

First Courses

Brussels Sprouts Salad

Sundown Summer Vegetable Soup

Crunchy Cheese Sticks

Tower Salad of Roasted Beets, Apples, Almonds, Goat Cheese, and Arugula

Tomato and Basil Soup

Soft-Shell Crabs

Brussels Sprouts Salad

1½ pounds Brussels sprouts

3 tablespoons olive oil

¼ cup fresh lemon juice

1 teaspoon chopped fresh thyme

⅓ cup chopped scallions

½ teaspoon salt

1⅓ cups hazelnuts, crushed and toasted

2 ounces grated Parmesan cheese

Wash the Brussels sprouts and remove the outer leaves. Shred them using a mandoline. Put them in a large mixing bowl. Add the oil, lemon juice, thyme, scallions, salt, and hazelnuts and toss to combine. Add the cheese and toss again to distribute evenly. Serve at room temperature.

SERVES 4 TO 6

Sundown Summer Vegetable Soup

2 tablespoons unsalted butter

½ cup chopped shallots

3 cloves garlic, chopped

1 cup diced carrots

1 cup diced zucchini

1 cup diced yellow squash

1 (28-ounce) can stewed Roma tomatoes, diced

2 cups homemade chicken broth

1 teaspoon chopped fresh thyme

1 tablespoon chopped fresh basil

Salt and freshly ground black pepper

8 ounces asparagus, trimmed and cut into ¼- to ½-inch pieces

Grated Parmesan cheese

Melt the butter in a medium saucepan over medium-high heat. Add the shallots and garlic and cook until they start to brown, 3 minutes. Add the carrots, zucchini, and squash and cook until tender, 4 to 5 minutes. Add the tomatoes and cook for about 5 minutes. Add the broth, thyme, and basil and season to taste with salt and pepper. Bring to a boil. Add the asparagus. Lower the heat slightly and cook until tender, 3 to 5 minutes.

Ladle into 6 soup bowls and sprinkle with cheese before serving.

SERVES 6

Crunchy Cheese Sticks

2 cups freshly grated Parmesan cheese

3 tablespoons paprika

1 sheet frozen puff pastry, thawed and cut in half

Preheat the oven to 400°F.

Combine the cheese and paprika.

Roll out one-half of the pastry. Sprinkle with one-half of the cheese mixture. Top with the other half of the pastry and sprinkle with the remaining cheese mixture. Press down with a rolling pin so the layers stick together. Cut into 1-inch strips and twist into cheese sticks. Arrange on a baking sheet and bake until golden, 15 minutes. Serve hot or at room temperature.

SERVES 6

Tower Salad of Roasted Beets, Apples, Almonds, Goat Cheese, and Arugula

I call this my Tower Salad. The presentation is an artistic challenge. It is not easy to keep the ingredients stacked vertically. Once it comes to the table, everyone seems to completely disregard the effort that went into keeping it upright. They just dig in and enjoy!

2 medium-to-large beets

½ cup sliced almonds

2 tablespoons unsalted butter

1 tablespoon honey

1 tablespoon plus ⅓ cup olive oil

10 ounces baby arugula

Salt and freshly ground black pepper

2 Gala apples, peeled and diced

2 teaspoons sugar

4 tablespoons balsamic vinegar

6 small cans or other molds

8 ounces goat cheese, at room temperature

Pea shoots or broccoli sprouts

Preheat the oven to 400°F.

Wrap the beets in aluminum foil and roast them for 1 hour. Let cool, then peel and dice them. Lower the oven temperature to 350°F.

Combine the almonds, 1 tablespoon of the butter, and the honey in a medium bowl. Spread the mixture on a baking sheet and roast for 15 minutes, stirring a few times. Let cool and break into pieces.

In a medium sauté pan, heat 1 tablespoon of the oil and add the arugula. Season with salt and pepper to taste. Stir until just wilted, about 3 minutes. Let cool.

In a medium sauté pan over medium heat, melt the remaining 1 tablespoon butter and add the apples. Cook over medium heat, stirring often, until the apples start to get soft, about 15 minutes. Add the sugar, a pinch of salt, and 1 tablespoon of the vinegar and continue to cook until the apples are very soft, about another 10 minutes. Let cool.

In a small bowl, whisk together the remaining 3 tablespoons of vinegar and ⅓ cup oil, and season with salt and pepper to taste.

Clean out six tomato-paste cans with the tops and bottoms removed or other similar molds. Make the salads by layering 1 tablespoon each of beets, arugula, apples, and goat cheese and about 2 teaspoons of almonds into each mold, drizzling each layer with some of the dressing. Continue to layer, ending with the almonds.

To serve, slide a spatula underneath each salad and place it on a serving dish. Carefully unmold the salad by pressing down on the salad with your fingers and lifting the mold with your other hand. Garnish the top with pea shoots or broccoli sprouts and drizzle with a little bit more dressing.

SERVES 6

Tomato and Basil Soup

1 medium onion, chopped

4 cloves garlic, chopped

7 to 8 tomatoes (beefsteak or plum)

2 quarts vegetable stock

½ bunch fresh basil

Salt and freshly ground black pepper

Pinch of sugar

½ cup low-fat milk

Grated Parmesan cheese

Sauté the onions and the garlic. Add the tomatoes. Add the vegetable stock, basil, salt, pepper, and a pinch of sugar. Bring to a boil, then lower the heat. Simmer for 10 to 12 minutes. Add the milk. Blend in a food processor. Serve at room temperature or chilled, with the cheese.

SERVES 6

Soft-Shell Crabs

This can also be a main course or a delicious treat for lunch.

FOR THE BEER BATTER

1 cup all-purpose flour

Pinch of salt

2 large eggs, separated

1 cup beer, at room temperature

2 tablespoons olive oil

FOR THE CRABS

3 cups vegetable oil for frying

1½ cups all-purpose flour

Salt and freshly ground black pepper

12 soft-shell crabs, cleaned

1 tablespoon olive oil

6 cloves garlic, minced

½ cup chopped shallots

6 tablespoons capers, drained

1 cup white wine

Juice of ½ lemon

1 tablespoon unsalted butter

Lemon wedges

TO MAKE THE BEER BATTER: In a large bowl, combine the flour, salt, and egg yolks. Stir in the beer and olive oil. In a separate bowl, beat the egg whites until stiff, then fold them into the egg yolk mixture.

TO MAKE THE CRABS: Heat the vegetable oil in a deep pot or deep fryer to 365° to 375°F. Season the flour with salt and pepper. Dredge the crabs in the flour mixture, then dip in the batter. Working in batches, fry the crabs until golden brown on both sides, about 1 to 2 minutes per side. Drain on paper towels.

Heat the olive oil in a sauté pan over medium heat, add the garlic and shallots, and sauté until translucent. Add the capers, wine, and lemon juice and bring to a boil. Cook the sauce until the liquid is reduced by half. Swirl in the butter. Serve 2 crabs per person, with the sauce and lemon wedges on the side.

SERVES 6

Tomato and Basil Soup

Main Courses and Side Dishes

Nana's Hungarian Beef Goulash

Crispy Potato Slices

Baked Stuffed Peppers Two Ways

Butterflied Breaded Veal Chops with Lemon Wedges

Crisp Oven-Baked Chicken Parmesan

Angel-Hair Pasta with Fresh Tomato Sauce

Salmon, Spinach, and Mushrooms in a Puff Pastry Crust

Miso Cod

Thai Coconut Black Rice

Seafood Paella

Vegetable Strudel

Nana's Hungarian Beef Goulash

I persuaded my mom to spend the summer with us at our beach house. We rented an adult tricycle for her with a lovely rattan basket in the back. I thought she might enjoy exploring the area this way. She loved the idea. I ran beside her while she practiced, just like my dad ran beside me when I got my first two-wheeler. By late afternoon, she was an accomplished rider, and from then on she took her dog along for the ride.

My mother used to tell my children stories about her childhood. During World War I, when the food supply was scarce in Vienna, her mother sent her and her sister off to spend the summers at her uncle's farm in Czechoslovakia. There the children could have their fill of cherries, peaches, plums, and apples, which they picked straight from the trees in the orchard. And there were raspberries and strawberries, and bushes of blackberries and blueberries, which they ate to their hearts' content. They drank fresh milk and ate the cream straight from the dairy. They slathered their freshly baked, still-warm farm bread with the butter and cheese made from the milk of the cows and the goats that they tended. The chickens, ducks, and geese from the farm provided all the fresh eggs and poultry. My children and I never tired of listening to my mother as she shared those happy moments from her childhood with us.

The Austro-Hungarian empire included Austria, Hungary, Bosnia and Herzegovina, Croatia, the Czech Republic, Slovakia, Slovenia, and parts of Italy, Montenegro, Poland, Romania, Serbia, and the Ukraine. Cultures mingled, and recipes were shared. That's how my Viennese mother ended up with a delicious Hungarian beef goulash recipe.

6 pounds lean beef stew meat, cubed

2 tablespoons safflower oil

5 large onions, sliced

6 cloves garlic, chopped

½ tablespoon paprika

3¾ cups water

3 cups beef stock

1 bay leaf

1 pound carrots, sliced

2 cups peas

Salt and freshly ground black pepper

Chopped fresh parsley

3 tablespoons all-purpose flour

In a large pot over medium heat, quickly sauté the beef until browned. Once the beef has browned, remove it from the pot and add the oil, onion, and garlic to the pot and sauté with a little paprika. Return the beef to the pot and sprinkle with the remaining paprika. Add 3½ cups of the water, the beef stock, and the bay leaf. Simmer, covered, for 2 hours.

Add the carrots and the peas, and cook until tender. Season with salt, pepper, and parsley to taste.

Mix the flour with the remaining ¼ cup water until smooth, and stir the mixture into the stew to thicken it. To make a more rustic stew, add torn pieces of crusty bread.

SERVES 6 TO 8

Crispy Potato Slices

In the farmer's field behind our house, there were rows of corn on one side, rows of potatoes on the other, and cantaloupes in the middle. I recall digging for potatoes there with Nana. Some potatoes were humongous—a single one could feed four people—and others were tiny dots. One doesn't usually find these potatoes in the markets. I've never tasted anything like those lightly sautéed potatoes sprinkled sparingly with kosher salt. This style of potato always reminds me of my mother's cooking.

6 large russet potatoes, peeled, sliced ½ inch thick, and parboiled

1 tablespoon salt

1 teaspoon freshly ground black pepper

2 tablespoons unsalted butter

2 tablespoons olive oil

½ cup finely chopped onion

In a large bowl, toss the potatoes with the salt and pepper.

Heat 1 tablespoon each of the butter and oil together in a large skillet over medium heat, and sauté the onion for about 5 minutes. Add the potatoes to the pan and toss gently to combine with the onions. Cook over medium heat until golden brown on the bottom, about 7 minutes. Flip the potatoes over, adding the remaining 1 tablespoon each of butter and oil, and cook on the other side until golden brown. Cut the pancake into six wedges and serve immediately.

SERVES 6

Baked Stuffed Peppers Two Ways

My mother made stuffed peppers with ground beef, rice, raisins, and tomato sauce. I converted this meat meal into something the vegetarians in our family enjoy very much. I do two styles: one is with couscous, garbanzo beans, and dried fruit for a Middle Eastern flavor; and, the other is with orzo, tomatoes, olives, and feta cheese for more of a Greek taste.

Middle Eastern Style

6 red bell peppers

6 yellow bell peppers

3 tablespoons olive oil

2 cloves garlic, minced

1 medium onion, finely chopped

1 green bell pepper, seeded and chopped

½ teaspoon turmeric

½ teaspoon ground cumin

2 teaspoons ground cinnamon

Salt and freshly ground black pepper

3 cups cooked couscous

½ cup dried currants or chopped dried dates

1 cup cooked garbanzo beans

½ cup pine nuts

¼ cup chopped fresh parsley

Vegetable stock

1 cup shredded sharp cheddar cheese

Preheat the oven to 350°F.

Wash the outsides of the red and yellow peppers. Cut off the tops and reserve. Remove and discard the seeds and membranes. Place the red and yellow peppers, along with the tops, in a large pot and cover with salted water. Bring to a boil, then simmer for 5 minutes. Drain and set aside to cool.

Heat the oil in a sauté pan and cook the garlic, onion, and green pepper for 8 to 10 minutes. Add the turmeric, cumin, cinnamon, and salt and pepper to taste and cook for 2 to 4 minutes to combine the flavors. Remove from heat and stir in the couscous, currants, garbanzo beans, pine nuts, and parsley. Season with more salt and pepper. The mixture should be moist but not too wet. If dry, add the stock ¼ cup at a time.

Spoon the mixture into the cooked peppers. Put the caps on top of the peppers. Place the peppers in a greased glass baking dish. Cover with aluminum foil and bake for 45 minutes. Remove the foil and sprinkle with the cheese. Bake until the cheese has melted, then serve hot.

SERVES 12

Greek Style

6 red bell peppers

6 yellow bell peppers

3 tablespoons olive oil

2 cloves garlic, minced

1 medium onion, finely chopped

1 green bell pepper, seeded
and chopped

3 cups cooked orzo

3 tomatoes, chopped

2 cups crumbled feta cheese

½ cup Kalamata olives, pitted
and chopped

½ cup pine nuts

1 tablespoon dried oregano

¼ cup chopped fresh mint

Juice of 1 lemon

Salt and freshly ground black
pepper

Vegetable stock

Preheat the oven to 350°F.

Wash the outsides of the red and yellow peppers. Cut off the tops and reserve. Remove and discard the seeds and membranes. Place the red and yellow peppers, along with the tops, in a large pot and cover with salted water. Bring to a boil, then simmer for 5 minutes. Drain and set aside to cool.

Heat the oil in a sauté pan and cook the garlic, onion, and green pepper for 8 to 10 minutes. Remove from heat and stir in the orzo, tomatoes, 1½ cups of the cheese, olives, pine nuts, oregano, mint, and lemon juice. Season with salt and pepper. The mixture should be moist but not too wet. If dry, add the stock ¼ cup at a time.

Spoon the mixture into the cooked peppers. Put the caps on top of the peppers. Place the peppers in a greased glass baking dish. Cover with aluminum foil and bake for 45 minutes. Remove the foil and sprinkle with the remaining cheese. Bake until the cheese has melted, then serve hot.

SERVES 12

Butterflied Breaded Veal Chops
with Lemon Wedges

My mother made the best Wiener schnitzel ever. When I was a child, it was my favorite meal. My husband loves it too, but he really prefers his veal on the bone. So I adapted my mom's recipe to make him happy. Once I mastered it, he would ask for it once a week.

A good tip I learned along the way: Move and shake the pan that the veal is cooking in so that the crust is puffed up like a dome above the meat. Also, try a mix of basic bread crumbs with panko bread crumbs if you feel like adding a little extra crispiness.

Start this meal with a healthy, colorful, summer vegetable soup. It balances the veal nicely, as does a side of steamed fresh vegetables. Or try the Viennese Cucumber Salad to start (see page 46).

6 veal loin chops, with bone, butterflied, and pounded to ⅛ inch thickness

Salt and freshly ground black pepper

Garlic salt and paprika (optional)

1 cup all-purpose flour

3 large eggs, beaten

2 cups bread crumbs (baguette, matzo, or panko)

Canola oil for shallow frying

Lemon wedges

Season the veal with salt and pepper and (if using) the garlic salt and paprika. Fill three separate shallow bowls with flour, eggs, and bread crumbs. Dredge the chops in the flour, then dip them in the eggs and coat with the bread crumbs.

Heat a large deep skillet over medium heat and add ¼ inch of the oil. Add the veal and cook, shaking the pan gently back and forth, bathing the veal in the oil. Cook until golden brown, about 3 minutes on each side. Serve with lemon wedges.

SERVES 6

Crisp Oven-Baked Chicken Parmesan

When the children were little, I would stay at the beach with them during the week, and Ralph would drive back to the city to work. I would prepare for his weekend return by cooking certain favorite foods ahead of time. This freed me up to spend precious hours with Ralph and the children on the beach. Chicken Parmesan was the great weekend favorite as a lunch or dinner meal. To avoid deep frying, I baked the breaded chicken, added a layer of tomato sauce, then topped it all off with a layer of mozzarella, which melts in the warm oven. At mealtime I would pile the chicken on a large platter and place it in the middle of the table as the main event, served with a side dish of angel hair pasta. Even though I made an enormous amount, it never lasted through the weekend!

Nonstick spray oil

1 cup all-purpose flour

Salt and freshly ground pepper

Paprika

Lawry's garlic salt

2 eggs, beaten

1½ cup panko bread crumbs

2 whole chickens, cut into 10 pieces each

1 pound mozzarella cheese, sliced

2 cups Fresh Tomato Sauce

Preheat the oven to 350°F. Spray a pan large enough to hold all the chicken with spray oil. Mix the flour and seasonings together in a shallow bowl. Put the eggs and bread crumbs in two additional shallow bowls. Dredge the chicken pieces, first in the flour, then in the eggs, and last in the bread crumbs. Place the pieces in a large roasting pan. Bake until golden, 30 to 35 minutes, turning the chicken when browned on bottom side.

Place the sliced mozzarella on top of the finished chicken and pour the fresh tomato sauce on top. Remove from the oven when the cheese has melted and the sauce is piping hot. Place on a large platter and serve.

SERVES 8 TO 10

Angel Hair Pasta with Fresh Tomato Sauce

2 pounds fresh plum tomatoes

16 ounces uncooked angel hair pasta

6 tablespoons olive oil

3 cloves garlic, chopped

Pinch of crushed red pepper

½ medium onion, finely chopped

Salt

3 tablespoons chopped fresh basil

Peel the tomatoes by scoring the skin of each with a sharp knife. Place the tomatoes in a pot of boiling water and boil for approximately 1½ minutes, then remove them with a slotted spoon and plunge them into cold water. The skins will easily slip off. Chop and set aside.

In the meantime, cook the pasta al dente in boiling, salted water for 8 to 10 minutes; drain. Heat the oil in a saucepan over medium heat, then add the garlic and red pepper. Sauté until the garlic turns slightly golden. Add the chopped onion and sauté for another 2 minutes. Add the tomatoes and cook for 5 minutes. Add salt to taste. Add the chopped basil and a little more olive oil, then toss with the pasta. Serve.

SERVES 4 TO 6

Salmon, Spinach, and Mushrooms in a Puff Pastry Crust

When the children were young, a fish dinner was not the most joyfully anticipated meal of the week. It was a challenge to entice my children to eat it. The first time I had salmon en croute was at a fancy, formal dinner event. The pastry crust that covered the fish made me think that I might have found a way to interest my children in eating fish. After all, they liked animal crackers, so why not some salmon encased in what looked like a giant animal cracker fish? I immediately started experimenting with the pastry dough at home. Some of my attempts were more like misshapen Pop Art pieces. Eventually, I ended up with a pretty masterfully created likeness of a fish. What a way to sell my kids on the idea that eating food fresh from the sea was not such a bad idea after all!

1 (10-ounce) package frozen chopped spinach

1 teaspoon unsalted butter

2 mushrooms, chopped

2 shallots, finely chopped

2 pieces frozen puff pastry, 12 inches by 6 inches, thawed

1 (1¼- to 1½-pound) salmon fillet (tail piece, about 12 inches long)

½ teaspoon salt

Freshly ground black pepper

1 large egg, beaten

Preheat the oven to 425° F.

Cook the spinach in boiled salted water for 1 to 2 minutes. Press out as much liquid as possible.

Melt the butter in a large pan over medium heat. Sauté the mushrooms and shallots in the butter until translucent, then add them to the spinach.

Roll out both pieces of pastry lengthwise to 14 inches. Place on a baking sheet and put in refrigerator.

Season the salmon with salt and pepper.

TO ASSEMBLE: Trim the pastry to look like a fish and be sure to include a "tail" of pastry. Spread the spinach and mushroom mixture evenly over the pastry. Place the seasoned salmon on top of it. Brush the edge of the pastry with egg. Top the salmon with the second puff pastry piece. Cut into the same fish shape and press down on the edges to seal them. Brush the pastry lightly with the egg. Refrigerate for 15 minutes.

Bake the fish for 15 minutes, then lower the oven temperature to 350°F and bake for another 10 minutes. The fish is done when a thermometer inserted into the center reaches 140°F. Bring to the table on a platter, slice, and serve.

SERVES 4 TO 6

Miso Cod

6 (6-ounce) cod fillets

½ cup white miso

¼ cup dark brown sugar

1 teaspoon toasted sesame oil

Preheat the broiler.

Rinse and pat dry the fillets. Combine the miso, brown sugar, and sesame oil in a bowl until the sugar dissolves. Brush each fillet with the miso mixture. Marinate for up to 2 hours. Place the fish on a baking sheet, then into the broiler until the glaze caramelizes, about 4 minutes. Remove the fish from the broiler and drizzle the rest of the miso mixture over it. Reduce the oven temperature to 375°F and cook for another 5 minutes.

SERVES 6

Thai Coconut Black Rice

1½ cups black sticky rice, soaked in water for at least 6 hours or overnight

2 cups unsweetened coconut milk

1½ cups water

¼ teaspoon salt

Drain the rice and put it in a saucepan with the coconut milk, water, and salt. Bring to a boil. Cover and lower the heat. Cook over low heat until most of the liquid has been absorbed, 8 to 10 minutes. If the rice is not tender, add more water or coconut milk. Serve hot.

SERVES 4 TO 6

Seafood Paella

I like to serve this salad with chilled, steamed asparagus spears and artichoke hearts in a lemon vinaigrette.

¼ cup olive oil

1¾ pounds chicken breast, cut into 10 pieces, washed and patted dry

1 large Spanish or yellow onion, diced

3 cloves garlic, minced

3 ripe Roma tomatoes, chopped

Salt and freshly ground black pepper

¼ teaspoon paprika

3 cups uncooked short-grain rice

3 teaspoons saffron threads

4 to 6 cups chicken stock

1 pound shrimp, peeled and deveined

12 clams, scrubbed

12 mussels, scrubbed and debearded

1 pound calamari, cleaned and sliced into rings

3 lobster tails, split

6 lobster claws

1 pound chorizo sausage, browned

1 cup frozen peas, thawed

1 red bell pepper, roasted, peeled, and cut into strips

Lemon wedges

Heat the oil in a 14-inch paella pan or wide skillet over medium heat. Brown the chicken on all sides. Remove the chicken from the pan and set aside. Without cleaning the pan, add the onion and garlic and sauté until translucent. Add the tomatoes and cook until the mixture is caramelized, about 10 minutes. Season with salt and pepper to taste and add the paprika.

Add the rice to the pan and stir until the grains are coated. Add the saffron and stock and simmer for 10 minutes. Move the pan around so the rice cooks evenly. Do not cover or stir.

Add the shrimp, clams, mussels, calamari, lobster, chicken, and sausage. Simmer without stirring until the rice is al dente and the mussels and clams have opened; discard any mussels or clams that do not open.

Scatter the peas on top and continue to cook until the liquid is absorbed. Let rest for 5 minutes before serving, garnished with the roasted-pepper strips and lemon wedges.

SERVES 6

Vegetable Strudel

Try beginning this meal with Curried Butternut Squash-and-Apple Soup (see page 41). The strudel can also be served as an appetizer or a side dish. If served as a main event, I complement it with plenty of exciting, colorful vegetables.

¼ cup olive oil

3 cloves garlic, chopped

1 onion, chopped

8 ounces edamame, shelled

8 ounces frozen chopped spinach, thawed and squeezed dry

4 tomatoes, chopped

2 large eggs, beaten

4 ounces fresh buffalo mozzarella, sliced

5 to 6 sheets frozen phyllo dough, thawed

5 tablespoons butter, melted

Preheat the oven to 400°F.

Heat the oil in a large sauté pan over medium heat and sauté the garlic and onion until translucent. Add the edamame, spinach, and tomatoes and cook for 8 to 10 minutes. Let cool. Add the eggs and cheese and stir well.

Using 5 to 6 full sheets of phyllo, lay the first one flat, the long side in front of you, and brush it with melted butter. Layer the second sheet, and brush with butter. Continue stacking. Place the filling in a log shape, 2 inches from the bottom side closest to you, leaving 2 inches at each end.

Fold the 2 inches of phyllo on each end over the log. Roll the edge of phyllo closest to you up and over the log, completely enclosing it as you roll up the rest of the phyllo sheet. Place it on a baking sheet, seam-side down. Brush with butter. Bake until the phyllo is golden and crispy, approximately 15 to 20 minutes. Let cool slightly and slice.

SERVES 6

Desserts

David's Ice Cream and Brownie Cannonball

Nana's Rum-Laced Brownies

Pound Cake

David's Ice Cream and Brownie Cannonball

On Saturday evenings after the children were bathed, fed, and dressed in their Dr. Denton pajamas and little plaid robes, we would all gather in the living room to watch *The Love Boat* and *Fantasy Island* on television. During "intermission," the children would race off to the kitchen to climb on chairs to scale the kitchen counters, and rush to prepare their favorite snacks to share with us. The children were like a team of oompa loompas on an assembly line, tossing Twinkies, Mallomars, red Twizzlers, and Mr. Salty pretzel bags down to one another, squealing with delight, raiding the freezer for ice cream and sorbets, sharing in the fun of concocting treats of malteds, shakes, and ice-cream sodas. Then, in relay style, they'd run back and forth into the living room with their arms full of supplies. We would have contests to taste whose ice cream soda was the best. Sprinkles, nuts, and maple syrup would enhance the chocolate syrup, ice cream, and Pepsi or 7-Up, just a few of the basic ingredients in these concoctions. This recipe is one of the winning combinations that I had prepared ahead of time knowing everyone would love it. Please note that adults and children alike all nod in approval when I serve this dessert!

1 quart vanilla ice cream

½ quart chocolate sorbet

½ quart coffee ice cream

6 pieces brownie, with nuts, broken by hand into chunky bits

1 cup chopped mixed nuts: walnuts, almonds, pistachios, or almonds

½ cup semisweet chocolate chips

Remove the ice cream and sorbet from the freezer and allow them to soften, about 20 to 30 minutes. Place the ice cream and sorbet in a bowl and add the brownie, nuts, and chocolate chips. Mix to just incorporate. Spoon the mixture into a pudding bowl, smooth the top, and freeze until hard, at least 2 hours.

To serve, run the outside of the bowl under hot water to loosen the frozen ball. Place a plate on top of the bowl and invert it. If you feel like an extra delight, serve with chocolate sauce and whipped cream.

SERVES 6

Nana's Rum-Laced Brownies

Ralph loved Nana's brownies so much that he offered to put a brownie department in his stores for her! That way he would not have to wait all the way until his October birthday when she would make another batch for him to savor and devour. David remembers how we treasured Nana's brownies so much that we rationed them in small morsels over as many weeks as we could stretch them! When my mother stayed with us in the Hamptons, we were so happy that she made the brownies for us all summer long.

FOR THE BROWNIES

1 cup (2 sticks) salted butter

6 ounces unsweetened chocolate

3 cups granulated sugar

6 eggs

3 teaspoons vanilla extract

2 cups all-purpose flour

1½ teaspoons baking powder

Pinch of salt

1½ cups chopped walnuts

FOR THE GLAZE

6 tablespoons (¾ stick) salted butter

4 ounces unsweetened chocolate

¼ cup confectioners' sugar

2 teaspoons vanilla extract

Rum or brandy to taste

Walnut halves

Preheat the oven to 375°F.

TO MAKE THE BROWNIES: Grease and flour a 9-by-13-inch pan. Melt the butter, chocolate, and sugar in the top of a double boiler over simmering water. Beat the eggs with the vanilla. Sift together the flour, baking powder, and salt. Mix all the ingredients together and stir in the walnuts. Pour the mixture into the prepared pan. Bake until a toothpick inserted into the center comes out clean, 35 to 40 minutes. Allow to cool before frosting.

TO MAKE THE GLAZE: Melt the butter and chocolate. Mix in all the other ingredients except the walnuts, then spread the frosting evenly on the cooled brownies. Cut into squares and decorate with the walnut halves. Refrigerate for 1 hour.

MAKES 12 BROWNIES

Pound Cake

Pound cake is incredibly versatile. Ralph likes his with ice cream and chocolate syrup. I like mine with cut strawberries and chantilly or whipped cream. I also like to serve Viennese coffee with it, which is a favorite of mine.

3 cups all-purpose flour

1 teaspoon baking powder

3 cups (6 sticks) unsalted butter, at room temperature

3⅓ cups sugar

1 teaspoon vanilla extract

8 eggs, at room temperature

Preheat the oven to 350°F. Sift the flour and baking powder together. In another bowl, cream the butter, sugar, and vanilla until light and fluffy. Add the eggs one at a time. Gradually add the flour to the mixture. Divide the batter between two 9-by-5-inch loaf pans. Bake until a toothpick inserted into the center comes out clean, 45 to 55 minutes.

SERVES 10 TO 12

(First row, left to right): The Hotel Astor in New York City was the largest hotel in the world in its time. Frank Lloyd Wright's Taliesin West, Scottsdale, Arizona. (Second row, left to right): The Carera Beach House by Antonin Raymond. The gardens of The Orchard. The Shrine of the Book designed by Frederick Kiesler and Arnold Bartos to house the Dead Sea Scrolls.

(Third row, left to right): Gardens, designed by Stanford White for Frances Breese Miller. The Otto Spaeth House, designed by Gordon Chadwick and George Nelson. William and Fred Muschenheim in the Hotel Astor roof garden, New York, 1905. The interior of architect Robert Rosenberg's East Hampton home. (Fourth row, left to right): Antonin Raymond's home in Montauk. The Shelter at Frank Lloyd Wright's Taliesin West. (Fifth row, left to right): A George Nelson apartment decorated with Herman Miller furniture. Architect Frederick J. Kiesler with his space sculpture Galaxy. Peter Blake's Pinwheel House.

The Architects

The natural landscape that has inspired modern artists to express themselves by communing within the boundless arena of nature has also influenced the architects. By exploring the architecture that evolved in the area, we continue to trace the weave of the rich tapestry that is the Hamptons today.

To begin, American modernist architect William Muschenheim (son of the wealthy co-owner of the Hotel Astor) designed simple bathhouses in Hampton Bays in 1930 that were connected to the beach by wooden walkways. These bold, geometric expressions were unadorned and rose up from the dunes. Practical and stylish, they expressed nonconformity and independence. Moreover, they were relatively affordable.

The artist and designer Frances Breese Miller grew up in her wealthy father's white plantation-style Southampton home, named The Orchard and designed by Stanford White. Miller, however, was influenced by the modern architecture of Europe to draw up a design for her own home, which consisted of a rectangular-box-shaped, flat-roofed structure built into the side of a dune. Erected circa 1933, it was dubbed The Sandbox, and thought to be one of the first modern houses on the east coast.

The architect Antonin Raymond, an émigré from Prague, built a house on the Montauk cliffs around 1939. The Carera Beach House reflected elements of his experiences training under Frank Lloyd Wright and the period he spent in Japan building modernist houses. Raymond's work incorporated natural materials into the wild ocean landscape.

"Weekend Utopia" stated: "Early experiments in beachfront living by Raymond, Miller, Muschenheim and others set the stage for what was to come after the hiatus of WWII, when a new generation of artists and architects would discover the Hamptons' landscape and interpret it in their own ways." After World War II, modernism began to take a decisive hold in America. Architectural modernism could easily be adapted for use in designing summer homes. Architects of the time created modern beach houses as a statement of personal freedom. The ocean beach offered a blank canvas, a place of dunes and light, and a simple background for the geometry and modernity of the new architectural movement.

Among the first architects to come to the East End were Europeans Pierre Chareau, Frederick Kiesler, Paul Lester Wiener, and Peter Blake, and Americans Tony Smith, Robert Rosenberg, and George Nelson—all of whom were inspired by the landscape to create structures that were in keeping with the beach, dunes, and farmlands. Modern architects left their imprints like sculptures as they reinterpreted the Hamptons landscape.

While abstract expressionists presented their interpretations of the area by painting on mural-size canvases, architects translated their experiences of the landscape by creating sculptural buildings that were strategically positioned in relationship to the environment. The modern architect integrated the house within the landscape.

The artist Robert Motherwell commissioned a house and studio in East Hampton in 1945. His friend Chareau, one of Europe's greatest modernist architects and the designer of the Maison de Verre in Paris, built him a "Quonset Hut"–type house. A departure from the existing architecture in the Hamptons, it was "the first modern house," marking "the beginning of a trend in the Hamptons away from the Traditional to an International, Modernistic style," according to James Brooke. The design was based on an eccentric semicylindrical system of prefabricated shelters, which could be transported easily and erected out of a kit that was developed during the early part of World War II by navy architects due to the shortage of building supplies. The house demonstrated the possible use of war surplus and industrial materials in residential construction. With its openness, easy flow, and structural elements, the house, left exposed and unfinished, seemed to be an extension of Motherwell's own work.

In 1946 Philip Johnson completed the Eugene Farney House in Sagaponack. It was one of the first flat-roofed houses on eastern Long Island and was described as "a rectangular box of vertical cedar siding, with outdoor decks set within the overall volume. A main living space is in the center, family bedrooms are on one side, and a kitchen and extra bedroom are on the other," by Paul Goldberg, author of *The Houses of the Hamptons.*

In the 1950s and '60s, the modernist direction inspired the new architecture in the Hamptons. Modern architects experimented with expressive and exciting forms that expanded on the concept of the rectangle with ocean-facing glass walls. By the 1950s, small plots of farmland were being sold off in the Hamptons for beach houses. Those constructed nearest the ocean were the most reflective of the new architectural movement. The "International Style" described

homes comprising unified, flowing living spaces rather than the typical separate rooms of traditional houses. The simple décor and easy maintenance made a household staff unnecessary.

After the war, *Life* magazine wrote, "Rising incomes, longer vacations, more holiday weekends, and the constantly improving highways all tempted the wage-earner to seek out a change of scenery for his leisure time." The concept of the weekend house was born. Modern houses ideal for weekend living were built along the oceanfront. The dunes in Bridgehampton, inlets of Springs, potato fields in Water Mill, and bluffs of Montauk would now become the perfect locations for the modern house.

Glass houses were particular favorites, for all but eliminating the boundary between the inside and the outside. Architects were free to create structures with no rigid conventional rules and site them within the wild, natural landscape. The most famous examples of the new style were Mies van der Rohe's 1950 Farnsworth House in Plano, Illinois, with its "glassed-in space supported by the most minimal of structural elements," flat roof, and stone floor; and Philip Johnson's Glass House, built in New Canaan, Connecticut, in 1949, which was all glass except for cylindrical bathrooms and kitchen cabinets. Johnson built another glass house in which living and dining occurred along a glass-enclosed central breezeway with two private pavilions, one on either side. This style of house became somewhat of a template for the beach houses that would soon follow in the Hamptons.

Architect and artist Tony Smith was interested in complex crystalline shapes and became famous for his geometric sculptures. In 1951 he planned and built a hexagon-shaped house for the artist Theodoros Stamos in Greenport, Long Island. It was erected upon pillars and crisscrossing trusses to maximize ocean views.

The architect Robert Rosenberg designed and built a beach house in East Hampton in 1952 on Further Lane. It was an all-glass building set back under a deeply protruding flat roof. Thus, another nontraditional house had been built in the Hamptons.

German architect Peter Blake created the Pinwheel House for himself in 1953 in the town of Water Mill. He built it in a potato field on four-foot pillars in order to see above the dunes to the ocean beyond. It was a 2,400-square-foot box-shaped construction made of wood, glass, and concrete block. The walls were like barn doors on steel tracks but could be moved in any number of ways to open up the house to views of the ocean. The act of pulling one of the sliding walls into place was a kind of "action architecture," like the "action painting" that his friend Jackson
Pollock was doing at the time. When completely open, the interior was fully exposed to the landscape; when closed, its box shape offered protection against inclement weather, like hurricanes. It was a variation on Mies van der Rohe's glass pavilions in Germany.

Keeping faith with modernism, Blake built simple modern beach houses from 1954 to 1962. With Julian Neski as his partner in 1956, he built a house that *Life* magazine called a "flat cigar box on stilts" in Bridgehampton. In 1959 the architect Guy G. Rothenstein built himself a cube that floated above the dunes on Fire Island. He also experimented with plastics in the construction of prefabricated housing systems and interior items for mass housing. His idea was to furnish these houses with molded plastic furniture for easy cleaning and space saving.

During the late 1950s and early '60s, Andrew Geller designed unique houses called "summer-use playhouses" that broke away from the typical architectural geometric cube. These one-of-a-kind houses for people of moderate means were built as economically as possible. One such house was a small, portable box-shaped unit with a fold-up deck and could be set up on stilts inexpensively. It was a bachelor pad that could be folded up and moved at a moment's notice. Geller's free-form beach houses were customized to the owners' needs. He gave the structures pet names like "Butterfly," "Box Kite," and "Milk Carton." The beach house he designed in Westhampton in 1959 was a "double box-kite connected by two diamond-shaped forms [hovering 'on point'] above the Westhampton dunes. A free-standing fireplace was set in the central living space between the two diamond-shaped pods. [The house had] three compact bedrooms, which he called bunk rooms, a bathroom and tucked-away storage spaces," wrote Alistair Gordon.

In 1955, as a counterpoint to the modern trend of the times, George Nelson and Gordon Chadwick built a house in East Hampton in a style that borrowed from the architectural firm of McKim, Mead, and White, namely that of the Low House, built in 1887. Paul Goldberger, the *New York Times* architecture critic, described the Low House as "one of the greatest houses of the nineteenth century in part because of the brilliance with which it wed abstraction to traditional style." Nelson and Chadwick built their modern version of the Low House. The exterior was shingled with a gabled roof, reverting back to a traditional era and definitely challenging the trend of the flat-roofed beach houses that had been the recent rage in the Hamptons. The look of the 1880s cottages and the saltbox-style houses of the old colonial era, but now with modern interiors, became the new modern. Hence, in the 1960s, "traditional" houses that either existed or were to be built were modernized with glass panels, ramps, and interior space reallotments.

Architect Carl Koch was influenced by Walter Gropius and Marcel Breuer of the Bauhaus school. In the early 1950s, Koch developed the idea of "Techbuilt houses— affordable prefabricated mass-produced homes that had architectural distinction."

It was not until the early 1960s that fifty of his revolutionary units were built on Long Island. For the first time ever, a two-part television program was created to encourage young families to order their own assembly-line prefabricated homes for delivery and construction on site within days. Partitions created rooms, and their number, size, and location could be manipulated to suit the needs of each family.

In the late 1960s, a group of young architects was "invited by Arthur Drexler, the director of MoMA's architecture department, to meet informally in the museum's board room to talk about their work." The meetings continued with only five of the original invitees in attendance: Peter Eisenman, Michael Graves, Charles Gwathmey, John Hejduk, and Richard Meier. After their work appeared in the Museum of Modern Art, they became known as "The New York Five," "The Fives," or "The Whites." However, Gwathmey, Hejduk, and Meier were the only three of the group who were working on projects in the Hamptons at the time, along with Barbara and Julian Neski, who were also influenced by Le Corbusier. The new houses

they designed became abstract objects that floated above the landscape. These geometric sculptures had integrity of their own and stood bravely and defiantly against their predecessors that had been so dependent on integration with the landscape. Photos of the new works were published internationally and open to critical analysis by the press. The Hamptons became the testing ground for each of the new young architects.

In 1964, at the age of twenty-seven, Charles Gwathmey designed what was to become the quintessential prototype for beach houses of the East Coast. Paul Goldberger described the Amagansett house, designed for Gwathmey's parents, as "a pair of buildings sheathed in vertical cedar siding, that rely heavily on primal geometries to create compositions of considerable intricacy." His design was "'modern' in the sense that it is austere and free of ornament. The composition of house and studio is organized around the diagonal." His design was subsequently copied by many, but the results never garnered the success of the original. Although only 1,200 square feet, it was an abstract sculptural object of artistic form that occupied its space with integrity and gave the sense of being a much larger structure. The house, which created an international sensation and became an architectural icon, is considered by many to be a masterpiece.

In 1964 the Neskis designed a series of detailed geometric summer houses in East Hampton to be respectful of the neighboring traditional houses. For example, they built a "saltbox[-style house] split in two. The living room, with a study/balcony, is a structure of its own, with a sharply pitched roof; a breezeway connects it to another pitched-roof structure containing the kitchen, dining room, and bedrooms," wrote Goldberger.

(First row, left to right): A casino designed by McKim, Mead and White, ca. 1881. The architect Charles Gwathmey. The Gwathmey home in the Hamptons. (Second row, left to right): The Farney House, designed by Philip Johnson. The Hunt family's summer home on Fire Island, designed by Andrew Geller in 1959. An interior of the Farney home.

(Third row, left to right): An interior of the Farney home. The Segal House of East Hampton, designed by Neski Associates. East Hampton home by Gordon Chadwick and George Nelson. (Fourth row, left to right): The interior of Robert Motherwell's Quonset Hut in 1985. Robert Motherwell in the house designed for him by Pierre Chareau in Amagansett. (Fifth row, left to right): New York's Pennsylvania Station, designed by McKim, Mead and White. Glass houses began to replace the more traditional style in the 1960s. The Theodoros Stamos home designed by Tony Smith.

For Richard Meier's first commission in 1966–67, he created a white-on-white geometric abstraction in East Hampton out of vertical cedar siding. The Hoffman House comprises two intersecting rectangles with a two-and-a-half-story triangular glass living room with a view facing toward nature on one side and closed to the road on the other. Then in 1969, Meier designed another house in East Hampton. The Saltzman House was described by Paul Goldberger as "a romanticized, highly picturesque adaptation of Le Corbusier's Villa Savoie," which was a "counterpoint to nature." As with the Hoffman House, the north side was almost blank, while the south side exploded with sundecks, curved walls, and receding space—all setting the stage for a most sought-after view of the ocean. Its overall size was in fact smaller than its appearance suggested.

In the early 1970s, Norman Jaffe set up an architectural practice in Bridgehampton. Unlike most of his contemporaries, who constructed generally vertical structures, Jaffe emphasized the horizontal integration of the house with the land. Inspired by a trip to Ireland, he created a compact, rough-stoned farmhouse set on a flat agricultural parcel of land. A long wall extended from the main house to give it a sense of presence, solidity, and scale within the environment.

The interior designer Ward Bennett created a number of beach houses in Amagansett and Southampton between 1969 and 1970. He is known for utilizing industrial designs, often incorporating huge geometric shapes, such as concrete slabs, and combining them with organic materials, thus calling to mind the relationship of the structure to nature.

From 1960 to 1980, the population of Southampton grew by 20 percent, and that of East Hampton by 27.8 percent. The Long Island Expressway became crowded with ever more traffic each weekend. With the advent of the Hampton Jitney in 1974, Manhattan and the Hamptons were connected by a direct express bus line. Soon dunes and potato fields were sprouting houses that often attempted, unsuccessfully, to emulate the style of Gwathmey, Meier, and the Neskis. Paul Goldberger wrote that the new structures "defy the ocean [and landscape]. They do not accept it: they challenge it." Rules concerning the environment and the zoning of new projects became necessary and were drawn up for the area.

Architectural historian Vincent Scully hailed the young architect Robert Venturi for his 1959 project for a proposed beach house, even though it was never realized. Outstanding about it was its extremely high, towering chimney located in its central living space. In a 1961 work inspired by Japanese style, Venturi built a house in East Hampton with William Short. It had a central fireplace, a traditional tea-house-shaped roof, and rustic beams.

Robert Rosenberg also designed a Japanese-style house, constructed in Quogue in the 1960s. In 1964 Rosenberg captured the essence of N'Debele, a South African village in the Transvaal, in the design of three separate "mud huts," for the textile designer Jack Lenor Larsen. The huts were fabricated out of concrete and erected on a twelve-acre compound in East Hampton. For other clients Rosenberg remodeled old barns that had been moved by him to beachfront sites. He also converted a disused church that had been relocated to East Hampton for writer Dorothy Norman. He designed the interiors to be modern while the exteriors maintained their unique vernacular expressions.

The houses that prevailed in the 1970s have been described by the journalist Alastair Gordon as "transitional" and "suggestive of traditional architecture." They were a mixture of the boxy modern style featuring open spaces, multilevel interiors, and multiple windows, while shingle siding gave the appearance of more traditional Hamptons-style homes. Architects such as Jaquelin T. Robertson, Alfredo De Vido, and Hobart Betts constructed Hamptons houses that reflected their own version of the hallmark style of the time: sloping roofs, shingled exteriors, and modern interiors.

Architect and historian Robert Stern built a house overlooking the ocean on the Montauk cliffs in 1972. He chose to look back to the original shingle-style homes, and then forward to the recent works of his mentor, Robert Venturi. The house's exterior reflected the style of the McKim, Mead, and White traditional house of 1887, while its interior was modern and open, and had multiple levels. By the late 1970s, architectural design had shifted as a result of Stern's stylistic influence. "By the 1980s, he had become the preeminent architect of 'traditional' houses on the South Fork."

In the 1980s the shingled houses of the turn of the century had once again become objects of admiration. Large, expensive new homes were being constructed that harkened back to the late 1800s and early 1900s. Resembling old estates in which separate rooms were defined again, houses in this neotraditional style were no longer experimental and innovative with the ambiguous open spaces of modern homes. Some exteriors were antiqued to give the impression that the houses were inherited. Windows were

symmetrical, and the Palladian window[16] became "an instant evocation of history, status, class and tradition. [It became the] ultimate antimodern emblem," wrote Gordon. As houses grew in size, so too did the necessity for growing higher and deeper privet hedges in order to protect these homes from scrutiny.

In 1985 Robert Motherwell's Quonset Hut was razed. The new property owners wanted to build an Adirondack-style house in its place. They commissioned architect Eugene Futterman, who had moved to the Hamptons in the late 1960s and was one of the most prolific architects in that area. Although he was trained as a modernist, his style became more traditional as taste shifted away from modernism to the more conservative neotraditional style, and he was among the first architects to reinterpret the shingle-style house. While the design for the exteriors of his homes came directly from architectural history, his interiors were reminiscent of his early modernist works, open and free-flowing.

Several other young architects continued designing in this vein. Among them were Eric Woodward, Francis Fleetwood, Gregory Zwirko, Stephen Levine, Carlos Brillembourg and Jonathan Lanman (of Brillembourg & Lanman), Paul Segal, and Michael Rubenstein.

Nevertheless, the trend to build bigger and more costly houses continued to rise in the 1990s. By 1998 the largest house in America to date was constructed in Sagaponack. The Rennert House, a 100,000-square-foot beach-side "Italian villa," was designed by the architect Mark Ferguson, built on sixty-five acres, and called "Fair Field." The "mega-mansion in once-quaint Sagaponack" was twice the

[16] Palladian window: a three-part window with a large arched center section flanked by shorter and narrower sections with square tops, popularly used in Renaissance architecture and other classical building styles.

(Clockwise from top left): The Rennert House, designed by Mark Ferguson. The Saltzman House, designed by Richard Meier. A classic Robert Venturi design. The Rosenblatt House of East Hampton exemplifies the traditional shingle style home. The H.R. Allen House, designed by Ward Bennett. The sixty-five acres of Fair Field. Venturi was inspired by Japanese style. Classic Palladian windows in Quogue, NY. The Hoffman House, designed by Richard Meier. Arakawa's first architectural project, the Bioscleave House.

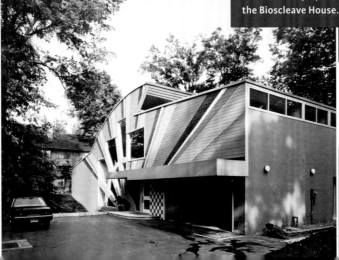

size of the White House and constructed out of white limestone and terra-cotta tiles," wrote Mary Cummings in *Sagaponak Revisited*. It consisted of "29 bedrooms, 39 bathrooms, a 164-seat theater, a restaurant-size kitchen,...[and] a garage that would accommodate more than 100 cars." The town administrators and local residents looked upon the permit application for a single-family residence with skepticism; however, it was ultimately approved by the town's building department and the Architectural and Historic Review Board.

In the late 1990s, the work of architects Tod Williams and Billie Tsien brought about a new interest in modern architecture in the Hamptons. Their 1998 Rifkind House in East Hampton saw a revival of the simplicity in design and connection to nature that were hallmarks of modernist architecture. The house consisted of four pavilions of wooden structures with floor-to-ceiling windows that were built around a courtyard and open to the landscape. The single-level construction offered a sense of spaciousness and did not impose upon the natural surroundings.

The developer Harry Coco Brown envisioned an enclave in the Hamptons before his death in 2005. The Houses at Sagaponack Project brought together a gathering of famous architects from around the world to design thirty-two moderately priced, ecologically considerate single-family homes on a 100-acre parcel of woodland in Sagaponack. Brown advocated a return to modernism and the creativity it had once inspired. He wanted to reverse the trend of building McMansions that had consumed so much of the agrarian landscape. With the help of his friend Richard Meier, Brown commissioned Stan Allen (dean of Princeton's School of Architecture) and other luminaries

such as Michael Graves, Zaha Hadid, and Philip Johnson. As of June 2009, seven out of the thirty-two houses had been built.

Many more architects have made and continue to make their contribution to the ever-changing Hamptons landscape. Some of the more recent notable architects are Fred Stelle of Stelle Architecture in Bridgehampton, Paul Masi of Bates Masi Architecture in Sag Harbor, and Bruce D. Nagel in Southampton.

Architecture in the Hamptons seems to be moving toward more ecologically sustainable and "life-enhancing" designs. The Project GreenHouse Hamptons, architect Edvin Karl Stromsten's experimental building in East Hampton, is built halfway into the earth with geothermal heating and cooling systems, and solar panels providing electricity. The house is anticipated to be almost energetically self-sufficient.

Artist Arakawa and his wife, Madeline Gins, profess that the home they designed for themselves will extend their lives. The "Bioscleave House"—or "Lifespan Extending Villa"—is their first architectural project. *The New York Times* wrote that it contains undulating concrete floors resembling "the surface of a vast, bumpy chocolate chip cookie." The objective of the uneven floor is to make people use their bodies optimally in order to maintain their equilibrium. According to Gins, keeping the inhabitants alert to their surroundings will stimulate their immune systems, and this in turn will keep them young.

Thanks to the relatively unspoiled landscape of natural beaches and a proximity to the cultural capital of the world, the Hamptons are the perfect showcase for furthering the experimentation and exploration of architectural development for the future of the world.

CHAPTER 4

Montauk

Our next foray into the Hamptons brought us to a lovely house in the still-remote area called Montauk. Montauk has always been attractive to those who prefer a more secluded environment. Artists and writers often purchased or rented homes there, and still do. John Lennon and Leonard Bernstein both had occupied this house before us.

The house was Japanese-inspired and built by one of Frank Lloyd Wright's disciples, the architect Antonin Raymond. The rooms had many panels of sliding-glass doors that stacked behind one another like shoji screens, with one wall open to nature and the sea, making certain spaces feel like indoor-outdoor rooms. Many doors opened directly onto the carpeted grass lawns, wooden decks, and stone pathways just beyond them. There was also a picturesque stone guest house that once functioned as a pony stable.

Dylan, Andrew, Ralph, David, and Ricky, Montauk, August 1989.

Ricky, Montauk, summer 1985.

Andrew, David, and Dylan, Montauk, summer 2005.

The main house was situated on top of the highest cliff in Montauk, which overlooked a great expanse of beach and ocean. It was dwarfed by giant black pines, which had been distressed from exposure to the storms and hurricanes that blow landward off the ocean from time to time in both summer and winter. The surviving pines assumed the shape of Japanese bonsai trees, only of enormous proportions.

The property was also landscaped with clusters of *Rosa rugosa* bushes bearing delicate pink blossoms. Wild blackberry brambles, beach plums, blueberry bushes, wild raspberry canes, and cherry shade trees dotted the dunes. Patches of tiny *fraises des bois* (wild strawberries) peeped out from the underbrush along the winding grass pathway that led down to the beach. Cypress and juniper lined the pebbled driveway. In the springtime, lavender blooms on vast walls of rhododendrons created tiny enclaves perfect for small seating areas for a picnic lunch, tea, or meditation. The effect evoked images of charming little houses and natural spaces that one might discover in Kyoto, Japan.

The dunes that we looked upon were part of a bird sanctuary. I was excited by sightings of piping plovers and terns. Hummingbirds, American goldfinches, chickadees, woodpeckers, and bluebirds would circle and play overhead. On our first day in the house, a little goldfinch mistakenly flew into our living room because we had forgotten to close the screen doors. After fluttering around for a short while, it landed on a wooden light soffit near the ceiling. It eventually found its way out again.

We enjoyed watching the piping plovers that raced along the beach, dodging the waves at the water's edge, and the terns that fearlessly nose-dived into the sea for their catch along its shimmering sunlit surface. Seagulls flew by quite often each day, and we witnessed the constant changes of the ocean, sky, and weather. We were very exposed to nature, and I became inspired to create meals that were healthful and respectful of her beautiful bounty.

Dylan and the Bunnies

Dylan dissected her cookies and muffins scientifically, separating chocolate bits, raisins, or nut chunks from the subject itself. She nibbled what she preferred like a bunny rabbit. Perhaps she could have packaged the bits she prized or even the leftover morsels as an item for her next creative sweets project.

When Dylan was a little girl, she had one black and one white rabbit, which she aptly named "Chocolate" and "Vanilla." She would mother them and be ever-present to see that they ate their bunny pellets and, of course, the treats that she offered them, like Oreo cookies, which they adored. Somehow she often found a way to slip away from the dining table. One minute she would be sitting right next to me, laboring over her peas and carrots, and when I turned back to glance her way, she would have disappeared by sliding beneath the table to escape to her beloved rabbits.

Rugby Loves Pretzels

Rugby, our dog of eleven years, was a most elegant mutt. He was part bearded collie and part English sheepdog. He would chase the cattle of Colorado but turn up his nose at the squirrels of New York's Central Park. Often during movie time at our Montauk home, Ralph would reward him with a pretzel treat, which Rugby delicately held between his upper and lower front teeth until he could settle in his own place and happily and noisily crunch it up. How Rugby loved pretzels!

The Montauk Blitz

Who in my immediate family can forget the infamous "Montauk Blitz," the chocolate, chocolate, chocolate mousse usually served as dessert after our last meal of the weekend, just before heading back to the city? It was as if our caretaker/ housekeeper/chef wanted us to have something to remember them by and, boy, it certainly did register with us.

VANILLA & CHOCOLATE

Ralph and Ricky, Montauk, August 1989.

Ricky and Rugby, Montauk, 1990.

Breakfasts

Egg in a Cup (Soft-Boiled Eggs)
Served with Toast Soldiers

Fresh-Start Morning Smoothies

Weekend Waffles with Good Old-Fashioned
Scrambled Eggs, Maple Syrup, and Sun-Kissed
Strawberries, Raspberries, and Blueberries with
Sweetened Light Sour Cream

Egg in a Cup (Soft-Boiled Eggs)
Served with Toast Soldiers

Each of my children liked his or her egg presented in a different way. One liked to leave most of the shell on, put the egg in a "chicken" cup, and use a favorite demitasse spoon to scoop the egg from the shell. Another loved it when I would draw a funny face on the shell and sit it in a little egg cup with feet on it. We had a collection of various egg-cup characters: a cowboy with boots, a deep-sea diver with flippers, and a duck with yellow webbed feet. The third child preferred the egg the way I did—and still do. In the case of the egg cup that has a large and small side, I remove most of the shell until, with the help of my little spoon, I can ease the egg from the rest of the shell and slide it into the larger end of the cup. Fresh pepper and an army of seven-grain toast "soldiers" (strips) stand by to be dipped into jelly, honey, or a little butter, and we are happy.

6 very fresh large eggs

Salt and/or fresh pepper to taste

Seven-grain bread, toasted and cut into strips

Take the eggs out of the refrigerator and let stand at room temperature for 30 minutes before cooking.

Heat enough water in a saucepan to cover the eggs by 1 inch. Bring the water to a boil. Gently lower the eggs into the boiling water. Bring to a simmer and cook for 4 minutes for a runny yolk, 6 minutes for a medium-boiled egg.

Immediately pour out the water and run the eggs under room-temperature water to stop further cooking, and to make them easier to peel.

Peel the eggs and serve with toast soldiers.

SERVES 6

Fresh-Start Morning Smoothies

Before an early morning bike ride or a run, even my children will tell you that it's good to have some fuel in your system. This is the time for one of our smoothies. They give you energy, and they are delicious!

Very Berry Smoothie

SERVES 1

¼ cup fresh blueberries, washed

¼ cup fresh strawberries, washed and hulled

¼ cup fresh raspberries, washed

¼ cup black currant juice

1 teaspoon honey

½ cup low-fat yogurt or soy milk

Banana Mango Bango Juice

SERVES 1

1 banana, sliced

1 mango, peeled and roughly diced

½ cup low-fat yogurt or soy milk

½ cup mango juice or orange juice

Sunrise Citrus Juice

SERVES 1 OR 2

½ cup fresh grapefruit juice

½ cup fresh orange juice

½ cup fresh strawberries, washed and hulled

½ cup crushed ice

For each smoothie, put all the ingredients in a blender and puree until smooth. Pour into a chilled glass and serve immediately.

Weekend Waffles

with Good Old-Fashioned Scrambled Eggs, Maple Syrup, and Sun-Kissed Strawberries, Raspberries, and Blueberries with Sweetened Light Sour Cream

What is it about waffles and eggs that elevates weekend mornings into something truly memorable and special? My family loves this special treat, which I serve with the scrambled eggs my family has come to love.

This is how I taught my children to make scrambled eggs. I like to briefly whip the eggs together with milk in a bowl. I whisk some butter around the inside surface of a hot skillet just to lightly coat it. Then I pour the egg mixture in. I sprinkle in a pinch of kosher salt and let the eggs settle before I start to scramble them. If I want to add anything to the basic egg, like American, cheddar, Boursin, or cream cheese, this is a good way for everything to start heating up and melting before I gently fold or "scramble" it all together. At the very end, I grind fresh pepper over them and add a teaspoon of chopped chives (optional), or I add them at the table.

Nonstick cooking spray or oil

1¾ cups all-purpose flour

1 tablespoon baking powder

1 tablespoon sugar

½ teaspoon salt

½ cup (1 stick) unsalted butter, melted

3 large eggs, well beaten

½ teaspoon vanilla extract

1½ cups low-fat milk

Spray a waffle iron with cooking spray, or lightly brush it with oil, and preheat.

Combine the dry ingredients in a bowl.

In a separate bowl, combine the butter, eggs, vanilla, and milk. Stir the wet ingredients into the dry, but do not overmix. Spoon one ladle of the batter onto the waffle iron. Cook until golden and crisp. Serve immediately. Repeat with the remaining batter.

SERVES 6

Luncheon
Seafood Frittata of Shrimp, Scallops, and Crabmeat with Green and Red Peppers
Sesame-Crusted Fresh Tuna Niçoise Salad
Mussels in Herbed White Wine Sauce
Greek Salad

Seafood Frittata of Shrimp, Scallops, and Crabmeat

with Green and Red Peppers

2 tablespoons olive oil

½ onion, sliced

½ cup diced red bell pepper

½ cup diced green bell pepper

Salt and freshly ground black pepper

3 to 4 cups mixed cooked seafood: shrimp, scallops, and crabmeat

½ cup asparagus tips, blanched

½ cup peas, blanched

¼ cup chopped fresh parsley

½ cup grated Parmesan cheese

4 large eggs, well beaten

Preheat the oven to 350°F.

Heat the oil in an oven-safe skillet over medium heat. Add the onion and peppers and season with salt and pepper; cook until soft, 5 to 8 minutes. Add the seafood and cook, shaking the pan, until it is warmed through. Turn the heat to low. Add the asparagus, peas, parsley, and cheese and season again. Pour the eggs into the pan. Bake for 15 minutes.

Cut into wedges and serve hot, warm, or at room temperature.

SERVES 4 TO 6

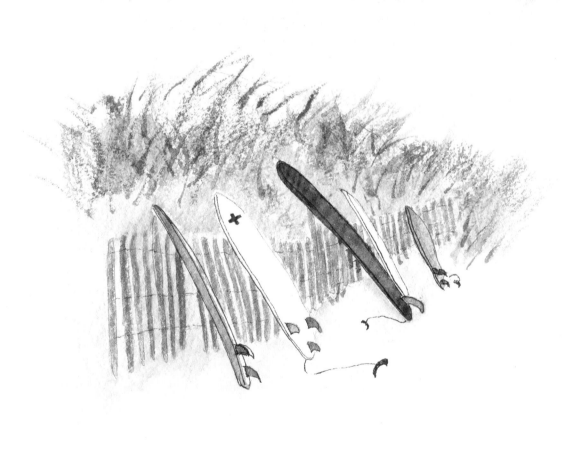

Sesame-Crusted Fresh Tuna Niçoise Salad

Although *niçoise* is the classic French name for this dish, I hesitate to call it that when it's more of a basic, fresh salad, and everything we use for it is bought locally. I buy the freshest sashimi-quality tuna from the nearby seafood market. The crunchy green beans, tiny new potatoes, frisée and romaine lettuce, and heirloom tomatoes are gathered from the garden or from my favorite farmstands. Even the eggs are farm-fresh organic! I like to serve this lunch with a cup of delicious, brightly colored soup on the side, and finish with a light, irresistible treat for dessert.

FOR THE TUNA

2 tablespoons white sesame seeds

2 tablespoons black sesame seeds

6 (4-ounce) pieces fresh tuna

3 tablespoons oil

FOR THE SALAD

1 head romaine lettuce, washed and torn into bite-sized pieces

1 cup ripe heirloom tomatoes, peeled, seeded, and diced

1 cup grated cucumber

1 cup diced red onion

1 pound fresh green beans, steamed until al dente

2 red potatoes, boiled and chopped

6 hard-boiled eggs, cooled, peeled, and quartered

4 teaspoons capers, drained

18 small green olives, pitted

18 small black olives, pitted

FOR THE DRESSING

½ cup red wine vinegar

6 tablespoons olive oil

2 cloves garlic, finely minced

¼ cup chopped fresh basil

Salt and freshly ground black pepper

TO MAKE THE TUNA: Combine the sesame seeds in a small bowl. Coat each piece of fish in the seeds and set aside. Heat the oil in a nonstick sauté pan over medium-high heat. Add the fish to the pan and cook for 3 minutes on each side. The tuna should still be pink inside. Transfer to a cutting board and cut into ¼-inch slices.

TO MAKE THE SALAD: Arrange the lettuce on 6 salad plates. Combine the tomatoes, cucumber, and onion and spoon them on top of the lettuce. Place 1 piece of grilled tuna on top of each plate. Arrange the beans, potatoes, and eggs around each plate. Scatter the capers and olives on top.

TO MAKE THE DRESSING: Combine all the ingredients and drizzle a little over each salad. Serve immediately.

SERVES 6

Mussels in Herbed White Wine Sauce

I like to serve this with Crisp Matchstick Potatoes (see page 110).

2 pounds mussels

2 tablespoons olive oil

2 small onions, diced

2 cloves garlic, minced

1 (28-ounce) can diced
 tomatoes, drained

½ cup white wine

½ cup clam broth

2 tablespoons chopped
fresh parsley

Scrub the mussels, removing the beards. Discard any that don't close when tapped.

In a large saucepan or Dutch oven, heat the oil over medium heat. Add the onions and garlic. Cook until fragrant and tender, about 4 minutes. Add the tomatoes. Bring to a boil, stirring for 3 minutes. Add the wine and clam broth and cook for 5 minutes. Add 1 tablespoon of the parsley and the mussels. Steam, covered, until all the mussels open, 7 to 10 minutes. Discard any unopened mussels. Sprinkle with the remaining 1 tablespoon parsley.

SERVES 4 TO 6

Greek Salad

⅓ cup olive oil

Juice of 1 lemon

1 teaspoon Dijon mustard

Salt and freshly ground
black pepper

2 heads romaine lettuce,
washed and cut into
½-inch strips

½ English cucumber,
sliced into ¼-inch strips

1 cup Kalamata olives,
pitted and halved

1 cup grape tomatoes,
halved

6 ounces feta cheese,
crumbled

½ cup finely chopped
fresh dill

Combine the oil, lemon juice, mustard, and salt and pepper to taste in a small bowl.

Combine all the remaining ingredients in a large bowl. Pour the dressing slowly over the salad and toss thoroughly. Serve immediately.

SERVES 4 TO 6

Mussels in Herbed White Wine Sauce

First Courses

Summer Rolls and Vegetable Bundles

Carrot and Spinach Terrine

Shrimp Rolls with Ginger-Chili Dipping Sauce

Yellow Gazpacho

Homemade Corn Chips

South Fork California Rolls

Sushi Rice

Summer Rolls and Vegetable Bundles

1½ teaspoons grated fresh ginger

2 small cloves garlic, minced

¼ cup fresh orange juice

3 tablespoons fresh lime juice

¼ cup soy sauce

12 snow peas, cut into 3-inch-long julienne strips

1 small carrot, cut into 3-inch-long julienne strips

1 scallion, cut into 3-inch-long julienne strips

1 red bell pepper, cut into 3-inch-long julienne strips

1 jicama, peeled and cut into 3-inch-long julienne strips

6 (8-inch) round Vietnamese rice wrappers

14 chives

In a large bowl, combine the ginger, garlic, orange and lime juices, and soy sauce. Add the snow peas, carrot, scallion, bell pepper, and jicama and toss to combine.

Submerge 1 wrapper in a large bowl filled with warm water. Let stand until soft and pliable but not limp, about 1 minute. Place the wrapper on a work surface. Mound ⅔ cup of the vegetable mixture at the end of the round closest to you. Fold in the sides of the rice paper and roll it tightly away from you. Repeat with the remaining wrappers and vegetable mixture, reserving the remaining vegetables and marinade. Cut each roll in half diagonally.

Strain the vegetables out of the marinade. Arrange the vegetables into 1-inch-diameter bundles, and tie each around the center with a chive.

Chop the remaining chives. Pour the strained marinade onto 6 individual serving dishes and sprinkle with the chopped chives. Arrange the summer rolls and vegetable bundles on the plates and serve with Ginger-Chili Dipping Sauce (see page 216).

SERVES 6

Carrot and Spinach Terrine

I also like to make this terrine using a layer each of salmon, cauliflower, and broccoli.

2½ pounds cooked carrots

1 cup fat-free sour cream

2 tablespoons all-purpose flour

2 teaspoons salt

4 large eggs

1 small onion, chopped

1 tablespoon safflower oil

10 ounces cooked spinach, drained and chopped

¼ teaspoon freshly grated nutmeg

10 ounces cooked broccoli

1 medium tomato, seeded and chopped

2 teaspoons rice vinegar

⅛ teaspoon freshly ground black pepper

Preheat the oven to 350°F.

Chop enough carrots to make ½ cup and reserve. In a food processor, puree the remaining carrots with ½ cup of the sour cream, 1 tablespoon of the flour, 1 teaspoon of the salt, and 2 of the eggs. Pour into a bowl and stir in the reserved carrots.

Sauté the onion in the oil over medium heat until tender. Process with the spinach, nutmeg, and remaining ½ cup sour cream, 1 tablespoon flour, 1 teaspoon salt, and 2 eggs. Pour into a separate bowl and stir in the broccoli.

Grease a 9-by-5-inch loaf pan. Pour half of the carrot mixture into the prepared pan, then half of the spinach mixture. Repeat to form layers. Cover tightly with aluminum foil. Bake the terrine in a roasting pan filled halfway with hot water (a bain-marie) for 90 minutes. Cool on a wire rack for 1 hour. Cover and refrigerate for 4 hours.

Mix the tomato with the vinegar and pepper. Invert the terrine onto a platter and top with the tomato relish. Slice the terrine to serve.

SERVES 6

Shrimp Rolls
with Ginger-Chili Dipping Sauce

FOR THE SHRIMP ROLLS

2 tablespoons olive oil

8 ounces large shrimp, shelled and deveined

3 cloves garlic, chopped

1 large carrot, grated

1 cup shredded cabbage

½ red bell pepper, seeded and finely chopped

½ yellow bell pepper, seeded and finely chopped

2 scallions, green part only, finely chopped

Salt and freshly ground black pepper

8 egg-roll skins

Canola oil for frying

FOR THE DIPPING SAUCE

1 teaspoon minced fresh ginger

3 tablespoons fish sauce

3 tablespoons fresh lime juice

3 tablespoons warm water

2 tablespoons sugar

1 clove garlic, crushed

1 fresh red or green chili, seeded and minced

½ cup chopped fresh cilantro (optional)

TO MAKE THE SHRIMP ROLLS: Heat the olive oil in a large sauté pan and add the shrimp and garlic. Cook gently over medium-low heat until the shrimp begin to turn pink. Transfer to a small bowl and let cool.

Mix together the carrot, cabbage, bell peppers, scallions, and salt and pepper to taste. Chop the shrimp and add them to the vegetables, along with the garlic and oil. Toss gently.

Lay out the egg-roll skins. Place about 2 tablespoons of the filling in the center of each skin. Fold in at the sides and roll from the bottom up. Seal the edges with a little water. Place seam-side up on a baking sheet lined with plastic wrap. Refrigerate (the rolls can be made to this point up to 1 hour ahead).

Heat 1 inch of canola oil in a large wok to 350° to 375°F. Using a slotted spoon, place the shrimp rolls in the oil and cook until golden on all sides, 5 to 6 minutes. Drain on paper towels.

TO MAKE THE DIPPING SAUCE: Combine all the ingredients together in a small bowl. Serve the sauce in small individual bowls with the rolls.

SERVES 8

Yellow Gazpacho

I like to serve this soup with Homemade Corn Chips. I provide garnish options such as scallions, sour cream, jalapeños, and red peppers. Guacamole is delicious with the corn chips.

2 cloves garlic, minced

1 white onion, chopped

1 medium cucumber, peeled and seeded

2 yellow bell peppers, seeded and chopped

2½ pounds ripe yellow tomatoes, peeled and seeded

1 cup juice of yellow tomatoes

4 scallions, chopped

¼ cup white balsamic vinegar

2 pinches of sugar

Salt and freshly ground black pepper to taste

Dash of Tabasco sauce

Blend all the ingredients in a food processor until roughly chopped and combined. Do not overprocess. Check the seasoning and adjust accordingly. Refrigerate for at least 2 hours before serving.

SERVES 6

Homemade Corn Chips

About 2 cups vegetable oil for deep frying

6 corn tortillas, cut into wedges

Salt

Heat 2 inches of oil in a heavy pot to 350°F. Working in batches, fry the tortillas until crisp. Remove with a slotted spoon and drain on paper towels. Sprinkle with salt and serve hot.

SERVES 6

South Fork California Rolls

California rolls are easy to make. The secret is perfectly vinegared sushi rice. Serve these with soy sauce, pickled ginger, and hot wasabi paste.

6½ sheets nori seaweed

4 cups cooked sushi rice

2 tablespoons toasted sesame seeds

2 avocados, not too ripe, pitted, peeled, and sliced

1 cup cooked crabmeat

1 English cucumber, seeded and cut into 4-inch-long strips

Pickled ginger

Wasabi paste or reconstituted powder

Soy sauce

Cover a bamboo sushi mat with plastic wrap. Place a sheet of the nori on this. Spread it with ¾ to 1 cup of the rice. Sprinkle sesame seeds evenly over the rice, pressing them into the rice. Flip the sheet over and remove the plastic wrap. The nori will now be faceup. Place the avocado, crabmeat, and cucumber horizontally on the seaweed near the edge closest to you.

Roll the bamboo mat forward, at the same time pressing the ingredients firmly inside into a roll shape. Remove the mat and cut the roll into 1-inch pieces. Repeat with the remaining nori sheets, rice, and filling.

Serve 1 roll per person with pickled ginger, wasabi paste, and soy sauce on the side of each plate, accompanied by steamed edamame.

SERVES 6

Sushi Rice

2¼ cups short-grain or sushi rice

4½ cups water

6 tablespoons rice vinegar

4 tablespoons sugar

2 teaspoons salt

Rinse the rice two or three times under cold water, until the water runs clear. Drain well to remove excess water. Put the rice and water in a large saucepan and bring to a boil. Lower the heat and cover. Cook for 15 minutes. Remove from heat and let stand for 10 minutes.

While the rice is cooking, combine the vinegar, sugar, and salt in a small saucepan and heat until the sugar and salt have dissolved.

Transfer the rice to a glass bowl and gently fold in the vinegar mixture. Each grain should be coated with vinegar. Wait until the rice is just warm before using it for the sushi.

MAKES 4 CUPS

Main Courses and Side Dishes

Baked Chicken with Mushroom Stuffing

Hamptons Beach Party Barbecue

Baby Lamb Chops

Fresh Applesauce

Good Old-Fashioned Garlic Mashed Potatoes

Chicken Under a Brick

Wild Rice Salad

Sesame-Crusted Tuna

Crispy Grilled Chilean Sea Bass

Asian Citrus Salad

Ditch Plains Clambake

Lobster, Avocado, and Mango Summer Rolls

Cold Sesame Noodles

Zucchini Stuffed with Black Beans, Corn, and Cheese

Cheese Quesadillas

Baked Chicken
with Mushroom Stuffing

This baked chicken recipe is very simple but also a crowd-pleaser, especially when I prepare it with this savory mushroom stuffing. I like to make my stuffing in a glass loaf dish.

1 tablespoon olive oil

1 clove garlic, chopped

2 shallots, chopped

1 cup sliced cremini mushrooms

1 cup sliced portobello mushrooms

½ cup chopped fresh parsley

Salt and freshly ground black pepper

2 cups day-old baguette, cubed

1 (3-pound) organic chicken

Preheat the oven to 350°F.

In a medium sauté pan, heat the oil over medium heat and add the garlic and shallots. Cook, stirring, until the shallots are translucent, 3 to 5 minutes. Add the mushrooms, parsley, and salt and pepper to taste and cook until the mushrooms are slightly softened, 1 to 2 minutes. Remove from heat and let cool to room temperature.

Combine the cubed bread and the mushroom mixture in a mixing bowl until the bread is moist.

Loosely pack the stuffing into the chicken. Put the chicken in a roasting pan, breast-side up, and roast until the juices run clear when a thigh is pierced, about 1 hour and 10 minutes. Scoop the stuffing onto serving plates. Carve the chicken and set pieces on top of the stuffing on each plate.

SERVES 6

Hamptons Beach Party Barbecue

Hamptons Beach Party Barbecue

When I want to cut back on calories but still enjoy a burger, I use a nice crispy romaine lettuce leaf instead of a bun to sandwich the burger, a slice of juicy tomato, and my usual condiments.

Ralph likes a delicious, juicy, old-fashioned crispy bacon cheeseburger (medium). But as far as he is concerned, it is not a barbecue unless there are frankfurters on the menu! He likes them with mustard and sauerkraut. He also likes a nice, juicy kosher pickle to be eaten by hand, and some crispy Hamptons fries on the side!

Everyone in our family loves a barbecue, and there are even those who eat "cheese dogs," which I've only recently discovered. I guess there is always something new to learn if one is open to experimentation.

Hamburgers

1½ pounds ground beef

½ medium onion, grated

½ teaspoon paprika

Freshly ground black pepper

¾ cup panko bread crumbs

1 egg, lightly beaten

2 tablespoons Worcestershire sauce

Salt to taste

6 hamburger buns

Mix all the ingredients thoroughly except the salt, which should be left until after the patties are cooked.

Make sure the mixture is cool. Divide and mold into six patties.

Cook on medium heat under the grill or on the barbecue to your preferred doneness. Salt to taste.

SERVES 6

Red Barn Turkey Burgers

1 large portobello-mushroom cap

1 tablespoon coarsely chopped shallot

3 tablespoons chopped fresh parsley

1½ pounds lean ground turkey

2 tablespoons olive oil

1 teaspoon Worcestershire sauce

Salt and freshly ground black pepper

6 thin slices white cheddar cheese

6 whole-grain rolls or English muffins

Avocado, tomatoes, onions, mustard, mayonnaise

Scoop out the underside of the mushroom cap. Cut the cap into 1-inch slices and put it in a food processor. Add the shallot and parsley and pulse until chopped. Transfer the mushroom mixture to a bowl.

Add the turkey, oil, Worcestershire sauce, and salt and pepper to taste. Mix (with your hands) until just combined. Divide into 6 patties, then put the patties onto a large plate, cover, and refrigerate for 30 minutes.

Grill the patties for 5 to 6 minutes on each side. Top with the cheese during the last 3 minutes of cooking. Serve on rolls or toasted muffins with an assortment of toppings.

SERVES 6

Veggie Burgers

4 cups shiitake mushrooms, sliced

Olive oil

1 cup chopped onion

2 cloves garlic, chopped

1 teaspoon grated fresh ginger

1 red bell pepper, seeded and chopped

1 yellow bell pepper, seeded and chopped

4 cups shelled edamame, blanched

1 (15-ounce) can chickpeas, drained

1 cup chopped scallions

1 cup finely chopped fresh parsley

1 large egg, beaten

Salt and freshly ground black pepper

6 hamburger buns

Preheat the oven to 350°F.

Sauté the mushrooms in a little oil and set them aside in a large bowl.

Sauté the onion, garlic, ginger, and bell peppers in a little oil over medium heat until tender, about 3 minutes. Add them to the mushrooms.

Coarsely chop the edamame and chickpeas in a food processor—don't overprocess. Add them to the mushrooms and stir in the scallions, parsley, and egg. Season with salt and pepper.

Shape the mixture into 6 patties and sauté them in oil over medium heat until golden on both sides. Finish cooking the burgers in the oven for 10 minutes. Serve on the buns.

SERVES 6

Baby Lamb Chops

When I had my little family, I learned quickly that a broiled lamb chop served as finger food was far more child-friendly than a rack of lamb. My children loved these lollipop-style lamb chops, because they could hold them in their hands while they chewed on the tender meat and the crispy bones. Nowadays, at our adult meals, our family will enjoy a rack of lamb together, but we also still take special pleasure in a "lollipop" dinner.

Lamb chops are best crispy on the outside and juicy pink in the middle. As an homage to my mother's cooking, I like to serve them with freshly made applesauce instead of the traditional mint jelly. After all, there is nothing like the aroma of apples and cinnamon sugar simmering on the kitchen stove to make a house smell like home. And, of course, nobody turns down garlic mashed potatoes.

2 racks of lamb, about 8 ribs each, chine bone removed by the butcher

Olive oil

Preheat the oven to 375°F. Remove all but a thin layer of fat from the lamb. In a large sauté pan, sear the lamb in oil on both sides for 5 to 10 minutes. Transfer to a baking pan and place in the oven. Roast for about 20 minutes for medium-rare. Cut into individual chops and serve immediately.

SERVES 6

Fresh Applesauce

8 assorted apples (McIntosh, Golden Delicious, Red Delicious, Rome, and Granny Smith), peeled, cored, and cut into large chunks

½ cup water

1 (3-inch) cinnamon stick

Place the apples, water, and cinnamon in a large, heavy pot and bring to a boil. Reduce the heat to a simmer, cover, and cook until the apples are very tender, about 15 minutes. Uncover the pot and cook for 5 minutes more to reduce liquid. Remove the cinnamon stick. Mash the apples with a fork into sauce.

MAKES 1 QUART

Good Old-Fashioned Garlic Mashed Potatoes

4 large Yukon gold potatoes, scrubbed, peeled, and cut into 1½-inch cubes

3 cloves garlic, minced

1 tablespoon olive oil

½ cup chicken broth

2 tablespoons unsalted butter

2 tablespoons sour cream

Salt and freshly ground black pepper

In a medium saucepan, cook the potatoes in boiling salted water until tender. Meanwhile, in a small saucepan over medium heat, sauté the garlic in the oil until translucent. Drain and mash the potatoes, adding the garlic, broth, butter, and sour cream. Season to taste and serve.

SERVES 6

Chicken Under a Brick

This crispy chicken is one of my favorites because it is delicate yet hearty.

FOR THE MARINADE

1 cup olive oil

Juice of 1 lemon

½ cup white wine vinegar

3 cloves garlic, crushed and finely chopped

1 tablespoon crushed red pepper flakes

1 tablespoon dried oregano

1 tablespoon dried thyme

1 tablespoon salt

FOR THE CHICKEN

2 small whole spring chickens

¼ cup vegetable oil for cooking

TO MAKE THE MARINADE: Combine all ingredients in a small bowl.

TO PREPARE THE CHICKEN: Place the chickens breast-side down and remove the backs by cutting along each side with poultry scissors. Cut off the first two sections of each wing and remove the rib cage with a boning knife—or have your butcher butterfly the chicken. Place the chickens in a bowl and completely cover with the marinade. Let them marinate in the refrigerator overnight.

When you're ready to cook, heat the vegetable oil in a skillet over medium-high heat. Place the chickens breast-side down in the pan and place a heavy foil-covered brick or a heavy cast-iron skillet on the chicken. Cook until juices run clear when a knife is inserted, about 15 minutes on each side. The skin will become crispy and golden brown.

SERVES 2

Wild Rice Salad

2½ cups chicken broth

1 cup uncooked wild rice

¼ cup chopped sun-dried tomatoes in olive oil

¼ cup pine nuts, toasted

8 Kalamata olives, pitted and halved

3 tablespoons chopped fresh flat-leaf parsley

¼ cup extra-virgin olive oil

2 tablespoons red wine vinegar

Salt and freshly ground black pepper

In a medium saucepan, bring the broth to a boil and add the rice. Turn the heat to low, cover, and cook until the rice is tender but still slightly chewy, 45 to 50 minutes. Drain and place the rice in a large bowl. Add the remaining ingredients and stir. Season to taste. Let the rice sit for at least 4 hours to allow flavors to develop. The salad can be prepared up to 1 day ahead and refrigerated.

SERVES 4 TO 6

Sesame-Crusted Tuna

I came across this dish while traveling. It's nice to surprise your family and guests with an occasional change from your regular menus. I welcome the challenge to create excitement and adventure at my own dining table through cooking a meal based upon the cuisine of a foreign land. I often think back on the fun I had choosing the desserts and the wine. I love to bring new recipes home with me from my travels. And if I cannot travel somewhere, I can always dream of the place and imagine what it must be like to be there, all the while sampling the regional recipes that I have attempted to make in my own kitchen.

FOR THE TUNA

3 tablespoons white sesame seeds

3 tablespoons black sesame seeds

6 (8- to 10-ounce) tuna steaks, ¾ inch thick

1 tablespoon safflower or canola oil

FOR THE DIPPING SAUCE

3 tablespoons soy sauce

2 tablespoons rice vinegar

2 tablespoons orange juice

1 teaspoon sesame oil

1 teaspoon grated fresh ginger

¼ cup chopped scallion greens

Wasabi paste or reconstituted powder

TO MAKE THE TUNA: Combine the sesame seeds in a small bowl. Coat each piece of fish in the seeds and set aside.

Heat the oil in a nonstick sauté pan over medium-high heat. Add the fish to the pan and cook for 3 minutes on each side. The tuna should still be pink inside. Transfer it to a cutting board and cut it into ¼-inch slices.

TO MAKE THE DIPPING SAUCE: Combine all the ingredients except the wasabi and serve alongside the tuna with the wasabi paste.

SERVES 6

Crispy Grilled Chilean Sea Bass

I like to serve the sea bass with beautiful, fresh Asian Citrus Salad. This meal also reflects our desire to eat healthfully.

1 cup duck sauce

1½ tablespoons soy sauce

1½ tablespoons mirin

1½ tablespoons teriyaki marinade

⅓ cup dry white wine

Juice of 1 lemon

3 cloves garlic, finely chopped

3 scallions, green part only, chopped

6 (8-ounce) Chilean sea bass fillets

3 tablespoons olive oil

In a medium bowl, whisk together the duck sauce, soy sauce, mirin, teriyaki marinade, wine, lemon juice, garlic, and scallions. Pour the marinade over the fish in a nonreactive dish, cover, and refrigerate for 2 hours.

Preheat a charcoal grill to high. Lightly oil the grill grate. Drain the fish and grill, flipping halfway, until a knife can be inserted easily into the center of the fish and the outside is crisp, 15 to 20 minutes.

SERVES 6

Asian Citrus Salad

FOR THE SALAD

1 cup shredded red cabbage

1 cup shredded white cabbage

2 cups baby spinach leaves

2 ribs celery, sliced

1 medium red bell pepper, seeded and cut into 1-inch pieces

1 medium yellow bell pepper, seeded and cut into 1-inch pieces

¾ cup mung-bean sprouts

4 scallions, white part only, chopped

1 (6-ounce) can mandarin oranges, drained, plus ¼ cup reserved juice

½ cup slivered almonds

FOR THE DRESSING

½ tablespoon finely grated fresh ginger

2 cloves garlic, minced

¼ cup safflower oil

½ teaspoon sesame oil (optional)

3 tablespoons rice vinegar

¼ cup finely chopped fresh cilantro (optional)

TO MAKE THE SALAD: In a large serving bowl, combine the cabbage, spinach, celery, peppers, bean sprouts, and scallions. Sprinkle the mandarin orange segments and almonds on top.

TO MAKE THE DRESSING: Whisk together all the ingredients in a small bowl. Drizzle the dressing over the salad and toss.

SERVES 6

Ditch Plains Clambake

All you need for success at this beach party is some good weather to share with family and friends. And bring along some happy music too!

6 russet potatoes, scrubbed

¼ to ⅓ cup olive oil

1 medium yellow onion, chopped

6 medium cloves garlic, chopped

1 cup dry white wine

2 cups clam juice

1 bunch fresh basil, chopped

1 bunch fresh parsley, chopped

2 leeks, thinly sliced and washed

2 tablespoons chopped fresh ginger

1 teaspoon saffron threads

1 teaspoon red pepper flakes

Salt and freshly ground black pepper

2 (1¾-pound) lobsters

1 pound king-crab or snow-crab legs

1 to 2 dozen littleneck clams, scrubbed

1 pound mussels, scrubbed

8 ounces large shrimp, shelled and deveined

8 ounces sea scallops

1 pound cod fillets

2 lemons, sliced

Preheat the oven to 400°F.

Bake the potatoes until tender, about 1 hour.

Heat the oil in a large pot over medium heat and sauté the onion and garlic until golden brown.

Add the wine and bring to a boil. Add the clam juice, basil, parsley, leeks, ginger, saffron, red pepper flakes, and salt and pepper to taste.

Add enough water—approximately 4 quarts—to cover the seafood when it's added. Bring to a boil. Drop in the lobsters and crab legs and boil for about 10 minutes.

Drop in the clams, mussels, shrimp, scallops, and cod. Cook for another 10 minutes. Remove the pot from heat and serve immediately, accompanied by sliced lemons, the baked potatoes, and Crisp Garlic Bread (see page 49).

SERVES 6

Lobster, Avocado, and Mango Summer Rolls

I like to serve this item with Cold Sesame Noodles. This fresh, light dish is the perfect, elegant summer treat.

FOR THE RELISH

2 mangos, pitted, peeled, and chopped

2 avocados, pitted, peeled, and chopped

⅓ cup mirin

⅓ cup rice vinegar

¼ cup finely chopped fresh parsley

Salt and freshly ground black pepper

FOR THE SUMMER ROLLS

8 (8-inch) round Vietnamese rice wrappers

2 avocados, pitted, peeled, and pureed

2 mangos, pitted, peeled, and cut into strips

3 (1½-pound) lobsters, cooked, shelled, and chopped

TO MAKE THE RELISH: Combine all the ingredients and set aside.

TO MAKE THE SUMMER ROLLS: Put the rice wrappers in a pan of water to hydrate and soften them, then carefully place them on a clean dish towel. Place some of the avocado puree in the center of each wrapper. Add some mango strips and lobster. Roll up like a burrito, tucking in the ends, and serve.

SERVES 8

Cold Sesame Noodles

½ (14-ounce) package dried soba noodles

3 tablespoons sesame oil

¾ cup natural peanut butter

2 scallions, chopped, plus more chopped greens for garnish

½ cup fresh lime juice

½ cup soy sauce

2 cloves garlic, chopped

2 tablespoons grated fresh ginger

½ cup warm water

¼ cup chopped roasted peanuts

Cook the noodles in boiling water according to the package directions. Drain and let cool.

Place the sesame oil, peanut butter, 2 scallions, lime juice, soy sauce, garlic, and ginger in the bowl of a food processor with the water and pulse to combine. Add more warm water if the consistency is too thick.

Stir the sauce into the noodles. Serve sprinkled with the peanuts and scallion greens.

SERVES 8

Zucchini Stuffed with Black Beans, Corn, and Cheese

We enjoy vegetarian dishes to balance with the fish, seafood, poultry, and meat dishes that we eat. Some of us are committed to vegetarianism, so we take pleasure in experimenting with the wonderful opportunities that are available to us to create exciting and fulfilling new meals.

2 (6- to 7-inch) zucchini or yellow squash, halved lengthwise

1 cup corn kernels

½ to ⅔ cup ricotta cheese

1 cup cooked black beans, drained

1 to 2 teaspoons chopped fresh chives

Salt and freshly ground black pepper

¾ cup shredded cheddar cheese

Preheat the oven to 350°F.

Scoop out the seeds from the squash, blanch the zucchini "shells" in boiling salted water, and drain.

Coarsely puree the corn and ricotta in a food processor. Transfer to a bowl and stir in the beans, chives, and salt and pepper to taste. Fill the squash halves with the mixture, mounding slightly, and cover with the cheddar cheese. Place in a buttered casserole dish and bake, covered, for 15 minutes. Uncover and bake until the topping is browned, 15 minutes longer.

SERVES 4

Cheese Quesadillas

¾ cup shredded cheddar cheese

¾ cup shredded Monterey Jack cheese

1 (4-ounce) can green chilies, chopped

¼ cup chopped onion

½ cup corn kernels

6 (10-inch) flour tortillas

Vegetable oil

Sour cream

Guacamole

Heat a charcoal grill.

Combine the cheeses, chilies, onion, and corn. Lay out 3 tortillas. Divide the cheese mixture among them, spreading evenly. Brush the grill grate with a little oil to prevent sticking. Place the topped tortillas on the grill and cook, moving them to make cross-hatched grill marks, until the cheese melts. Top with the remaining tortillas and flip over. Cook, moving them to mark the other side. Cut each quesadilla into 6 pieces. Serve hot with sour cream and guacamole.

SERVES 6

Desserts
Strawberry Soufflé
Chocolate Soufflé
Schaumrollen

Strawberry Soufflé

½ to ¾ cup granulated sugar

1 pint strawberries, washed, hulled, and pureed

5 egg whites

1 to 2 tablespoons confectioners' sugar

Preheat the oven to 350°F.

Butter the inside of a 1½-quart soufflé dish and sprinkle it with a little granulated sugar.

Pass the pureed strawberries through a sieve to remove the seeds. Add ¼ to ½ cup of the granulated sugar, depending on the sweetness of berries. Whisk the egg whites until stiff and add ¼ cup of the sugar. Beat until they become glossy and form stiff peaks. Stir a little into the puree, mixing well. Add the remaining puree to the meringue mix, folding together gently with a metal spoon. Gently spoon the mixture into the prepared dish. It should reach the top of the mold. Bake until puffed and browned, 25 to 30 minutes. Sprinkle the top with the confectioners' sugar and serve immediately.

A sauce of strawberry puree is an excellent accompaniment.

SERVES 4

Chocolate Soufflé

Superfine sugar

4 eggs, separated

3 teaspoons granulated sugar

3 ounces semisweet chocolate, finely grated

1 teaspoon all-purpose flour

Preheat the oven to 350°F.

Butter a large soufflé dish or 6 individual ramekins and sprinkle with a little superfine sugar, discarding any excess.

Beat the yolks and granulated sugar together. Add the chocolate and flour and beat until smooth. In a separate bowl, whisk the egg whites until stiff peaks form. Fold the whites into the yolk mixture until smooth.

Pour the mixture into the prepared dish(es) and bake for about 20 minutes. Sift some superfine sugar over the top of the soufflé(s) and serve immediately.

SERVES 6

Schaumrollen

This was one of my father's favorite desserts when he was a young boy. He introduced me to this Viennese dessert when my parents took me to Vienna for the first time. I, in turn, introduced my own children to Schaumrollen when I took each of them to Austria. It is a fantasy dessert. Everyone smiles when they eat it, reliving the innocence and pleasure of childhood. My daughter, Dylan, has now claimed Schaumrollen as her favorite dessert, and hopefully she will share this joyful treat with generations to come.

This Austrian dessert calls for the use of a special stainless steel tube. The tube resembles a cannoli mold but is bigger in diameter. Cannoli or cream-horn molds can be substituted.

FOR THE PASTRY

1 sheet frozen puff pastry, thawed in refrigerator

12 cannoli or cream-horn molds

1 free-range organic egg white, beaten

Chocolate sauce

FOR THE FILLING

3 free-range organic egg whites

2 cups light corn syrup

½ teaspoon salt

2 cups confectioners' sugar

1 tablespoon vanilla extract *

Preheat the oven to 350°F.

TO MAKE THE PASTRY: Roll out the puff pastry into a rectangle measuring 10 by 12 inches. Cut into twelve 1-inch-wide strips. Starting at one end of a cannoli mold (or the thinnest end if using cream-horn mold), wrap a pastry strip around the mold, overlapping as you proceed along its length. Slightly dampen the end so that it sticks to the mold. Place on a cookie sheet. Repeat until all 12 molds have been wrapped. Brush with the egg white and place in the oven to bake until golden, about 20 minutes. Remove from the oven and let cool completely. Remove from the mold and stuff with the filling. Coat with sifted confectioners' sugar or melted chocolate.

TO MAKE THE FILLING: In a large bowl, combine the egg whites, corn syrup, and salt. Beat with a mixer on high speed until thick, 10 minutes.

Add the confectioners' sugar. Beat on low speed until well blended. Add vanilla and mix until blended. This recipe may be frozen for later use. Remove from the freezer, allow to defrost, and stir until it is mixed. It can be refrigerated for up to 1 week.

* To make strawberry filling instead of vanilla, substitute strawberry flavoring for vanilla and add 1 or 2 drops of red food coloring.

MAKES 12 ROLLS

STEINBECK
EAST OF EDEN

the PARIS 35 REVIEW

DELTA OF VENUS
EROTICA BY
ANAÏS NIN

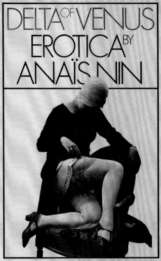

STEINBECK
Sweet Thursday

FAR TORTUGA

A NOVEL
PETER MATTHIESSEN

(Clockwise from top left): *East of Eden. The Paris Review,* winter 1953. George Plimpton, July 1979. *Delta of Venus. Sweet Thursday. Far Tortuga. Blue Meridian.* (Bottom): Poet, Frank O'Hara in Southampton, 1961. (Top): Art critic Harold Rosenberg at the Elaine Benson Gallery, Bridgehampton, 1975. *A Widow for One Year. Children of the Albatross. Laurence at the Piano* by Fairfield Porter, ca. 1953. *Self-Portrait* by Fairfield Porter, ca. 1972.

children
of the albatross

ánaïs nin

author of
"ladders to fire." "under a glass bell and other stories." etc.

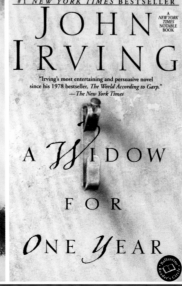

#1 *NEW YORK TIMES* BESTSELLER

A NEW YORK TIMES NOTABLE BOOK

JOHN IRVING

"Irving's most entertaining and persuasive novel since his 1978 bestseller, *The World According to Garp.*"
— The New York Times

A WIDOW
FOR
ONE YEAR

The Search for the
Great White Shark
BLUE MERIDIAN

Peter Matthiessen

The Authors

During World War II, Jeannette Rattray was an important interpreter of local experience to Hamptons readers. For more than fifty years, she wrote a weekly column called "Looking Them Over" for the newspaper of her husband, Arnold, *The East Hampton Star*. Rattray was able to tie in the events of the East End to the world at large during these years. A descendant of one of the oldest families in East Hampton, which had settled there in 1650, she also wrote a number of books about the East End's history and its maritime past.

John Hall Wheelock was a poet and contemporary of Jeannette Rattray's who spent most of his summers in East Hampton. He wrote eleven volumes of verse and a collection of criticism. As an editor at Scribner's for forty-five years, he was responsible for discovering and publishing younger poets, most notably James Dickey, May Swenson, and Louis Simpson.

In the 1940s and '50s, there was an influx of authors to the Hamptons. Harold Rosenberg, the writer, educator, philosopher, and art critic for the *New Yorker*, and his wife, artist May Natalie Tabak, came to Springs in 1943. French poet and essayist André Breton wrote a collection of poems, entitled *Jeunes Cerisiers Garantis Contre Les Lièvres* (1946), while spending time in Hampton Bays. Berton Roueche, a writer at the *New Yorker* and author of *Eleven Blue Men* (1954), *Feral* (1974), and *The Medical Detectives* (1980), took up permanent residence in Amagansett in 1948.

In the early 1950s, New York School poets John Ashbery, Barbara Guest, Kenneth Koch, and Frank O'Hara were introduced to the Hamptons when they visited or stayed to become long-term house guests of painter Fairfield Porter and his wife, Anne. James Schuyler, another poet, lived with the Porters from 1961 to 1973 and dedicated his first major collection of poetry to them.

Anaïs Nin, maverick of female erotica, was born in Paris but spent much of her childhood in Cuba. She made Sag Harbor her home in the 1950s.

The renowned author John Steinbeck came to Sag Harbor in 1953. He rented a house there while writing his novel *Sweet Thursday*, which was published in 1954. A year later, Steinbeck purchased this house, which he and his wife, Elaine, enjoyed until his death in 1968. Sag Harbor provided Steinbeck with inspiration for the characters in his book *The Winter of Our Discontent* (1961). Sag Harbor also became the launching point for *Travels with Charley: In Search of America* (1962), which described a year-long journey around the United States with Steinbeck's standard poodle.

When bohemian expatriates Peter Matthiessen; his wife, Patsy Southgate; and their friend George Plimpton returned from a sojourn in Paris, they brought with them the idea for a literary magazine that reflected an unconventional, nonconformist approach. They established *The Paris Review* in 1951 and continued to work on it when they relocated to the Hamptons. Matthiessen became a resident of Sagaponack in 1959. Matthiessen chose to live in a neighborhood that is somewhat of a writers' enclave. The authors John Irving, Kurt Vonnegut, James Salter, and Plimpton all lived close by. Vonnegut was a longtime Sagaponack resident/local who could be seen bicycling along the lanes with groceries in his basket. James Salter returned to the Hamptons in the 1980s after being stationed in Westhampton during his military service in the 1950s. He now lives in Bridgehampton.

The 1960s saw many more authors of distinction arriving to roost. Truman Capote had a saltbox house built for him near Gibson Beach in Sagaponack in 1961. It was in this house that the seminal work *In Cold Blood* was written in 1966. Capote enjoyed a very gregarious life, moving through literary circles as well as social ones. Among his friends were fellow Hamptonites Lee Radziwill and Gloria Vanderbilt (upon whom it is rumored the character Holly Golightly from *Breakfast at Tiffany's* was based).

The famous playwright Edward Albee found creative inspiration along the cliffs of Montauk, where he settled in 1962 while preparing *Who's Afraid of Virginia Woolf?* for Broadway. Albee has been a Montauk resident for more than forty years. In 1967 he created the Edward F. Albee Foundation, a retreat for writers, composers, and visual artists who come to Montauk during the summer months to live and create.

Willie Morris moved to Bridgehampton in 1967. At the time he was the youngest editor in chief of *Harper's* magazine. He mentored many other influential writers of the time, most notably James Jones, Capote, and Winston Groom. He and his fellow authors became a fixture at Bobby Van's Steakhouse in Bridgehampton. It was their meeting place and authors' club. "The place had dark mahogany paneling, a hardwood floor, booths, and a grand Victorian bar with mirrors, wooden carvings and bar stools," as described in *In the Hamptons.* Morris, Jones, Capote, Groom, Irving, Plimpton,

Vonnegut, Joseph Heller, and Irwin Shaw regularly held court at the bar.

The 1970s had its share of newly arriving literati. Betty Friedan, the feminist, activist, and writer of *The Feminine Mystique* (1963), began renting space on communes in different villages of the Hamptons in the early 1970s. By the mid '70s, she had found a home for herself in Sag Harbor. She was instrumental in the 1986 formation of the Sag Harbor Initiative: a forum for African-American and white residents from the area to discuss community issues.

Jones is best known for his novels *From Here to Eternity* (1951), *Some Came Running* (1957), and *The Thin Red Line* (1962). He moved to a Sagaponack farmhouse in the mid 1970s and started to write *Whistle* but died before completing it.

Heller began coming to the Hamptons in the 1970s, ultimately making Sagaponack his permanent residence in 1986. He is best known for his novel about World War II, *Catch-22* (1955). During his time in the East End, he wrote three novels: *Something Happened* (1974), *Good as Gold* (1979), and *God Knows* (1984).

Shaw, the playwright, screenwriter, novelist, and short-story writer, lived in Sagaponack. He is perhaps best known for *The Young Lions* (1948), *Fire Down Below* (1957), and *Rich Man, Poor Man* (1970).

E. L. Doctorow, a Sag Harbor resident, is an author celebrated for his evocative depictions of American life in the nineteenth and twentieth centuries.

Tom Wolfe has been a longtime Hamptons resident. In his novel *The Bonfire of the Vanities* (1987), a 1980s power couple from Manhattan vacation at their East Hampton home. From that novel comes the line "to own in the Hamptons is to have arrived."

In Cold Blood
Truman Capote

Joseph Heller
A novel
Good as Gold

THE YEAR'S MOST CONTROVERSIAL BESTSELLER

The Feminine Mystique

BETTY FRIEDAN

"The book we have been waiting for ... the wisest, sanest, soundest, most understanding and compassionate treatment of contemporary American woman's greatest problem...a triumph."
—ASHLEY MONTAGU

75¢

Breakfast at Tiffany's
A short novel and three stories by
Truman Capote

CATCH-22

A NOVEL BY

JOSEPH HELLER

The Kandy Kolored Tangerine-Flake Streamline Baby

TOM WOLFE

WHO'S AFRAID OF VIRGINIA WOOLF?

REVISED BY THE AUTHOR FOR THE 2005 BROADWAY REVIVAL

"Towers over the common run of contemporary plays."
—*The New York Times*

EDWARD ALBEE

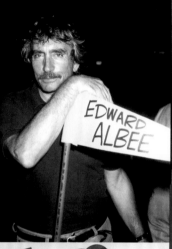

EDWARD ALBEE

Tom Wolfe

MAUVE GLOVES & MADMEN, CLUTTER & VINE

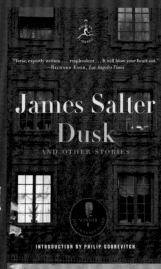

"Terse, expertly written ... resplendent ... It will blow your heart out."
—Richard Eder, *Los Angeles Times*

James Salter
DUSK
AND OTHER STORIES

WINNER

INTRODUCTION BY PHILIP GOUREVITCH

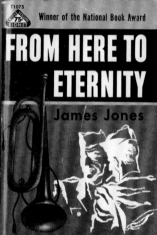

T1075

SIGNET 75¢

Winner of the National Book Award

FROM HERE TO ETERNITY

James Jones

A SIGNET TRIPLE VOLUME
Complete and Unabridged

(First column, top to bottom): *In Cold Blood*. American author E.L. Doctorow outside the Renwick Smallpox Hospital, 1994. *Good as Gold*. The Feminine Mystique. (Second column, top to bottom): *Breakfast at Tiffany's*. *Catch-22*. Tom Wolfe in his signature white suit, 1968. *The Kandy Kolored Tangerine Flake Streamline Baby*. (Third column, top to bottom): *Who's Afraid of Virginia Woolf?* Edward Albee during Scenery Greenery at Montauk Downs, 1986. *Mauve Gloves & Madmen, Clutter & Vine*. (Fourth column, top to bottom): *Dusk*. *From Here to Eternity*. *The Young Lions*.

IRWIN SHAW

The Young Lions

WITH A FOREWORD BY

(Top to bottom, left to right): Jaws. The 51st anniversary cover of Dan's Papers. Bluebeard. Tender is the Night. Further Lane.

Author, editor, and publisher Dan Rattiner has been a resident of the Hamptons for decades. He started his weekly newspaper, *Dan's Papers,* in 1960. At that time it was called *The Montauk Pioneer.* Rattiner has witnessed many aspects of life on the East End. His insider account of these experiences has given the reader a taste of life in the Hamptons. The weekly paper has been described as "the Bible of the Hamptons." Rattiner has also written two books about the Hamptons: *Who's Here* (1994) and *In the Hamptons* (2008). In 2007 he sold the newspaper but continues to be affiliated with it.

F. Scott Fitzgerald's characters in *Tender Is the Night* were based upon Sara and Gerald Murphy, whom he had met in the Hamptons and vacationed with in Europe during the war. Peter Benchley, in his book *Jaws* (1974), based the character of Captain Quint on Frank Mundus, a fisherman he encountered in Montauk in 1968.

Kurt Vonnegut offered us a vision of the Hamptons art scene in *Bluebeard* (1987). His main character, Rabo Karabekian, is a failed painter married to a well-to-do woman. He purchases abstract-expressionist art at a low rate to fill his home and becomes a curator/tour guide rather than an artist. Many familiar Hamptons locations are referenced in this novel.

In his 1988 book of short stories, *Dusk and Other Stories,* James Salter writes about a mother and her Dutch au pair in the Hamptons in a story called "Foreign Shores." In *A Widow for One Year,* John Irving's four protagonists are writers in Sagaponack.

The columnist James Brady of Amagansett has written four novels about the Hamptons: *Further Lane: A Novel of the Hamptons* (1997), *Gin Lane: A Novel of Southampton* (1998), *The House That Ate the Hamptons: Lily Pond*

Lane (1999), and *A Hamptons Christmas* (2001). The Hamptons have also been featured in Vincent Lardo's *The Hampton Affair* (1999) and *The Hampton Connection* (2000).

The Hamptons continue to enchant a coterie of authors and writers. Over the past three decades, playwright Joe Pintauro; authors Candace Bushnell, Jay McInerney, and Colson Whitehead; sportswriter/author Mike Lupica; journalist/screenwriter Nick Pileggi; and columnist/author Linda Bird Francke are among the many others who have been lured to the East End.

In 1948, sculptor and modernist painter Wilfred Zogbaum turned his backyard into the locale for a convivial game of softball for fellow artists like Jackson Pollock, Willem and Elaine de Kooning, Ibram Lassaw, Grace Hartigan, Howard Kanovitz, Conrad Marca-Relli, and Ludwig Sander. At the time, only two authors were allowed to infiltrate this artist-controlled game: Harold Rosenberg and Barney Rosset. However, by the 1960s, writers had joined in the by-now-legendary game. Vonnegut, Ken Auletta, Plimpton, Irving, Lupica, Jack Graves, Carl Bernstein, and Salter were regulars on the opposing side to the artists.

What started as a friendly game played and umpired among artist and writer friends grew over the years to include celebrities and people from many walks of life. Their ranks were joined by actors Roy Scheider, Eli Wallach, Dustin Hoffman, Alan Alda, Chevy Chase, Dina Merrill, Christopher Reeve, and Alec and Billy Baldwin; architects Charles Gwathmey and Ronnette Riley; athletes Pelé, Gerry Cooney, Wesley Walker, and Marty Lyons; filmmaker Ken Burns; journalists Ben Bradlee and Mort Zuckerman; musician Paul Simon; politicians Eugene McCarthy, Bill Clinton, Abbie Hoffman, Ed Koch, and Charlie Rangel; TV and radio personalities Peter Jennings, Mr. G., and James Lipton; and artists Eric Ernst, Eric Fischl, Bill Durham, and John Alexander.

In 1988 the game moved from its backyard origins to Herrick Park, located behind the stores in the center of town in East Hampton. The roster of players is made up of invited guests only, and it is broadcast on the local public-access television station. The game celebrated its sixtieth anniversary in 2008. For the past three decades, it has been organized by artist, actor, and restaurateur Leif Hope, who is also the manager for the artists' team. Journalist Ken Auletta is the manager of the writers' team. This annual event takes place in August and continues to be a tradition in the Hamptons.

In the 1980s, property in the Hamptons was relatively affordable compared with the price of land at popular European resorts or on the California coast, where land was scarce. The Hamptons offered a change and newness as yet unexplored. Prospective customers started buying property in the Hamptons as second homes as well as year-round residences. Real estate superseded tourism (which had clearly surpassed the once-principal occupations of farming and fishing) as the Hamptons' number-one industry. The Hamptons became an international playground populated by travelers drawn to the beautiful sandy beaches and the relaxed lifestyle. Publicity and notoriety increased over the years and seemed to entice people to congregate there. Celebrities attracted other successful types from business, medicine, government and academia to all of the arts including theater, music, fashion and film. The Hamptons became *the* place to go in the summertime, a trend that continues to this day, with no sign of stopping.

Because of my wonderful children, Andrew, David, and Dylan, there are special memories at the heart of this book. I see you in every home and at every table, filling the moments with your playfulness, your laughter, and your love. While I was writing this book, there were two new additions to our family, Paul and Lauren, whom I welcome with open arms.

Thank you to my mother and my mother-in-law for their legacy of recipes and cooking skills.

With pleasure I extend my thanks to the talented and generous Lee Ann Leichtfuss, Frances Mooney, and Mary Ruth Rera, the chefs who brought their recipes and their expertise at testing them to this book; and to Grace and Bill Ferrara, the original "Hamptons Homemakers," who cared for our family wonderfully for many years. Many thanks to my longtime staff, who traveled this journey with me—Michelle Lashley, Pilar Vergara, Elizabeth Eiel, and Freddy Martinez.

Thank you to Steve Murphy for introducing me to Melcher Media; and to Craig Smith for helping me to navigate the business of bookmaking. Thank you to Holly Dolce for your editorial expertise, and to Lynne Yeamans for your design input. Thank you Pamela Chirls of John Wiley & Sons for supporting the creation of this book.

Thank you to Sylvie Becquet of Paris for your loving photographic contribution, and to my dear friend Francoise Labro for introducing us; and to Ann Stratton for your outstanding food photography, Michael Pederson for beautifully preparing the delicious food every day of the second shoot, and Philippa Brathwaite for your creative spirit. Thank you to Devin Powell for your energy and invaluable help in facilitating this project; and to Michael Morelli, Doug Bihlmaier, John Devitt, and Carter Berg for your creative input.

I am especially grateful to JoAnne Tenzer and Jill Hurst for their commitment to this project. Jill, you have been instrumental in bringing it to fruition as a support and skillful liaison to everyone involved. This book has been years in the making—and JoAnne, you have been involved since the beginning. I appreciate your patience, your perseverance, and your comprehensive vision. Thank you.

It is a joy to create a life with my husband, Ralph, whose vision is the epitome of style. You are my greatest inspiration. I say this with abundant love and gratitude.

Recipe Index

Note: Italic page numbers refer to photographs.

Bibliography

"The Art," by Nicolai Ourousoof. *The New York Times,* New York, 2001.

Biography for James Rosenquist, by Pierrette Van Cleve. AskArt. Art Cellar Exchange, New York, 2011.

Guild Hall of East Hampton: An Adventure in the Arts, by Enez Whipple. Harry N. Abrams, Inc., New York, 1993.

Hampton Style: Houses, Gardens, Artists, by John Esten with Rose Bennett Gilberts, and photography by Susan Wood. Little, Brown & Company, Boston, 1993.

Hamptons Bohemia: Two Centuries of Artists and Writers on the Beach, by Helen A. Harrison and Constance Ayers Denne. Chronicle Books, San Francisco, 2002.

Hamptons Havens: The Best of Hamptons Cottages and Gardens, by the editors of *Hamptons Cottages and Gardens.* Bullfinch Press, New York, 2005.

The Hamptons: Long Island's East End, photography by Ken Miller, introduction by George Plimpton. Rizzoli, New York, 1993.

The Houses of the Hamptons, by Paul Goldberger. Alfred A. Knopf, New York, 1987.

In the Hamptons, by Dan Rattiner. Harmony Books, New York, 2008.

In the Spirit of the Hamptons, by Kelly Killoren-Bensimon. Assouline, New York, 2002.

"Is Ira Rennert Building a House or a Hamptons House of Worship?" by Frank DiGiacomo. *The New York Observer,* May 31, 1998.

"The List," *Hamptons,* Volume 29, Issue 1, May 25–May 31, 2007.

Long Island Country Houses and Their Architects, 1860–1940, edited by Robert B. MacKay, Anthony K. Baker, and Carol A. Traynor. W.W. Norton & Company, New York 1997.

Men's Lives, by Peter Matthiessen. The Rock Foundation, 1986.

"New Organization of/for Writers & Artists," by Debbie Tuma. *Dan's Paper.* Bridgehampton, New York, Volume XLVII, Number 12, June 12, 2009.

Selections From the Collection: Guild Hall Museum, foreword by Henry Korn and introduction by Lisa Panzera. Guild Hall of East Hampton, Inc., East Hampton, New York, 1998.

The Sixties: Young in the Hamptons, by John Jonas Gruen. Charta, Milan, Italy, 2006.

Studios by the Sea: Artists of Long Island's East End, text by Bob Colacello and photographs by Jonathan Becker. Harry N. Abrams, New York, 2002.

"Trend-Setting Quonset Hut is Demolished on LI," by James Brooke. *The New York Times,* New York, August 3, 1985.

Weekend Utopia: Modern Living in the Hamptons, by Alastair Gordon. Princeton Architectural Press, New York, 2001.

Who's Here: The Heart of the Hamptons, by Dan Rattiner. Pushcart Press, Wainscott, New York, 1994.

Photo Credits